7-26-74

OFFICIAL PHILOSOPHY

and

PHILOSOPHY

OFFICIAL PHILOSOPHY
and
PHILOSOPHY

JULES DE GAULTIER

Translated from the French by
Gerald M. Spring

PHILOSOPHICAL LIBRARY
New York

CONTENTS

I. Borrowing from anterior forms of experience.
II. Extension of the sovereignty of reason, in so far as
it designates the constant part of experience, to the
unstable and mobile part of experience which refers
to the moral phenomenon.

I. Extension of the sovereignty of reason, in so far as
it designates the forms of knowledge, to the domain
in which it would apply to the forms of action.
II. The illegitimate character of this extension. What
would be, amid the perspectives opened by the
forms of knowledge, the veritable form of action?

I. How one makes up a rational genealogy for reason.
II. A description of reason with a view to distinguishing it from the other activities of the mind produced
in its name. The moral and scientific modalities of
psychological activity.

PREFACE

The title of this work doubtless implies that it is a criticism of official philosophy and, as such, opposes to the latter another philosophy.

What, then, is official philosophy?

What is Philosophy?

The opposition that I established between the vital Instinct and the Instinct of Knowledge in my first work, FROM KANT TO NIETZSCHE, will serve to answer this double interrogation. Official philosophy is a philosophy of the vital instinct. Philosophy is the very expression of the Instinct of knowledge. The Philosophy of knowledge is concerned with knowing for the sake of knowing. The aim of this philosophy is identical with the activity itself, which is practised in it.

But, if the Philosophy of knowledge has no other aim than to satisfy the instinct rousing it, it only realizes this perfection of its nature at the end of a rather slow evolution. During a long historical period this instinct, at first without an object and destitute of any initiative of its own, little by little formulates itself, develops and grows until it attains that maturity of the aesthetic sense, in which it finds its satisfaction in the mere fact of knowing *how things happen*. In order to contemplate the laws of reality, to know *how things happen* and to find some joy in this spectacle, things must indeed take place in some fashion, there must be a reality. It is the vital Instinct that creates this reality in the course of a first phase of social evolution, in which it is master, where it commands and uses the Instinct of

7

knowledge as a means of realization, in the human milieu, of the ends which it proposes and tests in it. In this social environment, moreover, an objective end dominates all improvisation and weighs its value: it is the very fact of possible existence. It is a question of realizing conditions that render society possible. Now, this search is made gropingly, in the course of a thousand more or less fortunate experiments, which, before constituting a source of information for the future apt to inform on what it is expedient to do, amount to a series of adventures, of hazardous enterprises the success or failure of which alone measure the value after the accomplished event. When, during this improvisation, some opportune ways of being have been discovered which appear qualified to realize the social end, to render life in society possible, the vital instinct, changed into a social instinct, applies itself to inducing them in the individuals of the group. For this task it utilizes and enthralls the vital instinct, compelling it to invent, with the resources of its own industry, means of persuasion able to exert an influence on imaginations, one which engenders these opportune maners of being, the substance of morality.

Hence the Instinct of knowledge does not originally develop according to its own tendencies, but rather exerts itself as an involuntary and constrained collaborator of the social instinct. It does not apply itself to describing how things happen, but seeks with more or less luck to make them happen in the way desired by the social instinct. It is not as yet at the stage of contemplating reality, but engaged in fashioning it. In this capacity it not only invents mythologies, religions and philosophies, but fabricates means of seducing or intimidating the human mind in such a way as to incline it toward the chosen attitudes.

During a very long period it presumably happens that the steps urged by the social instinct are not the ones most apt to realize the social end. But taking things at an epoch nearer in time and supposing that, by the repeated action

8

of experiences, these steps, these ways of being are henceforth the most efficacious, it must still be said that the means invented by the instinct of knowledge to make them accepted and practised bear the marks of the epoch in which they were imagined. These steps, these manners of being, which one could designate by a general term "morality," do not receive their value from the reasons then invented for them; moreover, they derive their origin neither from the causality which was assigned them, nor from the fabulous genealogy composed for them. They get their value from the fact of having been propitious experiences. The mythologies and the fictions by which the instinct of knowledge established their credit by the use of means appropriate in the epoch in which they were employed, are really no more than provisional structures or scaffolding. Once the work is accomplished and the social edifice constructed, all that remains to be done is to withdraw them. But it is the last stage of the philosophical mind to recognize the purely historical character of their value and to discover the legitimacy of morality in the fact alone that it is the condition of existence, to derive it from experience as a means that has been successful.

In fact it occurs that these scaffolds, having for centuries been seen juxtaposed with the constructions they served to build, were taken for an essential part of the construction itself. Their nature was misunderstood. While they were no more than provisional means, they were taken to be indispensable supports, the withdrawal of which would cause the collapse of the edifice.

Thus the fate of morality was thought to be linked with that of certain beliefs, particularly with the destiny of the faith in free will, which was itself inserted so as to become a part of the spiritualistic mythology. Likewise, before knowing the veritable claims of morality, such as its effectiveness as a condition of existence, appreciating its utility, it had been deduced *a priori* in order to impose it with greater authority—first that of theology, then of rationalistic ideology, since the power to engender ideas and promulgate imperatives had been transferred from God to Reason.

The ensemble of these fictions, of these false causalities, may be summed up in a doctrine that is a spiritualistic rationalism. It is this doctrine that I have undertaken to criticize in the two studies making up this work. One is a critique of rationalism. In this I endeavor to show that this doctrine is a nominal usurpation, inasmuch as its name is borrowed from reason with a view to strengthening with its authority some imperatives, which grant reason an extraneous origin. By misusing the prestige of reason in behalf of certain moral theses, rationalism compromises reason and risks discrediting it. It is, therefore, in favor of reason that rationalism is criticized. This critique of rationalism, let there be no mistake, is a defense of reason. The second of these studies is more specially a censure of spiritualism. When I have brought out that spiritualism consists in an explanation of the World through two principles, mind and matter, which by definition do not admit of any community of nature, it will become sufficiently clear that this conception is equally criticized in the name of reason. I shall add that this censure is also undertaken in the name of a pure doctrine of the mind.

In the light of etymology, spiritualism is a betrayal. In the name of the spirit it introduces matter into the philosophical problem. Now, existence may be imagined and the world constructed in terms of matter. Such a doctrine can and does offer a great coherence, if one disregards the difficulty—it is a great one on reflection—of the making of thought, of the fact of consciousness, a mode of matter. But existence can likewise be imagined and the world constructed in terms of thought; with this new hypothesis the difficulty is less great, inasmuch as the two terms gratuitously differentiated by the spiritualistic postulate

10

may be reduced to one. Indeed it does not seem impossible to see in matter the ensemble of the modes, according to which thought represents itself to itself. Idealism, the doctrine of thought, is a monism by the same right as materialism. It implies the same coherence. Finally, it avails itself of all the scientific work accomplished on the hypothesis of matter. It is this doctrine of pure Idealism, which, in the light of the idea of Bovarysm, I opposed in the last part of this work to the spiritualistic rationalism of the school. *No existence can be conceived which does not have any consciousness of itself.* If the main proposition of idealism can be formulated in these terms, the maxim of Bovarysm is inscribed as its strict corollary in the following enunciation: *Existence conditioned by knowledge of itself, drawing from itself the object and the subject of this knowledge, necessarily conceives itself other than it is, in the indefinite and in the inadequate of relation.* This maxim shows its affinity with the aphorism of Auguste Comte: *All is relative, and that alone is absolute.* At the same time it shows among the cadres of Idealism and as one of its consequences the doctrine of the sovereignty of experience as the unique source of our knowledge.

The tendency of this little work therefore is, through the criticism of the official philosophy, to propose a new perspective, which the maturity of the instinct of knowledge nowadays permits one to realize: the positivistic perspective sanctifying, according to Auguste Comte's wish, the substitution of the positive spirit for the metaphysical spirit. It finally leads to this result, where it seems that the positive mind best counteracts that of the theological spirit, namely that all knowledge is necessarily inadequate to its object, so that *l'adaequatio rei et intellectus* taken by ancient philosophy to be the aim of its inquiry, far from marking the perfection of a state of knowledge, would reveal its chimerical nature, in such a manner that the inadequate character of scientific knowledge confessed by the

11

critical mind of the scholars and best philosophers of our time proclaims the value of scientific knowledge and attests that it is what it can and must be.

This accession of a philosophy of relation, of a positive philosophy, is something which the activity of speculative, literary and scientific thought has been preparing for almost a century. Hasn't the hour come to make a reality of it?

It certainly wouldn't be very reasonable to become indignant with the grossness of the means employed by ancient philosophy to found morality and induce the attitudes useful to social life. While engaging these two symbolic entities, the vital instinct and the instinct of knowledge which—need it be stated—amount to no more than algebraic formulas containing in a single easily wielded term two groups of multiple and concrete facts—I have indicated under what conditions this philosophy came about and what necessities it satisfied. At the time when it was formed there was no social experience in existence that could have been consulted in order to fashion and organize social life by profiting from its teachings. In all likelihood the vital instinct composed its substance and wove its texture in an improvisation, whose boldness and fecundity constituted its virtue. It was the rôle of the instinct of knowledge to invent fables apt to fortify by beliefs those among these improvisations which seemed to be successful. It is under these conditions that myths were invented; the religions, metaphysical systems and beliefs, to which they gave rise, play their part in the constitution of social morality, of the state of manners, in short of the aggregate of the ways of being permitting a society to live. Into this social experience, which today we are able to consult in our inquiry as to what are the modalities favorable to the life of human collectivities, there enter to a considerable extent theological elements, mythological elements, even elements produced by a prelogical mentality; thus with this free will, about which it is curious to find philosophers discussing whether it exists or does not exist at a time when the present forms of our logical mentality no longer permit us to discover a meaning in the word in which it is expressed; and thus with spiritualism, which poses the philosophical problem in such a manner that its solution would imply contradiction with the definition of the terms in which it is engendered. Now, if we are not to become indignant at the illogical character of these fictions, if it is even expedient to envisage gratefully the blind effort, which fashioned them in favor of the reality they helped to create, our gratitude could not be manifested better than by strengthening this social reality, in which they were fused and in which they are rediscovered in the tendency to the morality, which they engendered. Just as they, in order to bring about this morality, expressed themselves in forms apt to influence the manner of thinking of their epoch, we must promote means in keeping with the spirit of our own, so as to attain the same object, especially substitute for a tendentious causality, whose fictitious character the critical mind now discerns, recourse to experience. If the information afforded us in this way does not in all domains dispel the hazard concomitant with living, it does at least permit us from gleams projected by completed events to predict some of the contours of the future and to adopt expedient attitudes.

In order to preclude any misunderstanding I owe the reader one more precise statement in the way of clarification.

In the quest for fictions bequeathed to contemporary thought by vital instinct philosophies I have, in the course of this criticism, implicated University teaching. It couldn't be otherwise. As a matter of fact vital instinct philosophies reveal themselves, as soon as they are formulated, as social instinct philosophies. The social instinct in any collectivity has the state for its organ. Education is a function of this organ and it is dealt out through the mediation of the universities. Vital instinct philosophy, state philosophy, official philosophy, university philosophy, while not synonymous, are allied or approximate terms and it is indeed in university philosophy that those vestiges of the ancient fictions composed by the instinct of knowledge had to be rediscovered when, under the domination of the vital instinct, it was constrained to invent fabulous justifications for its decrees, to make people believe, instead of making them see, which is its proper function. That is the way in which things happened and the work of M. Parodi, an account and an appraisement from the standpoint of university philosophy, of the philosophical systems of these last thirty years, this work, which furnished a pretext, as an antithesis, for the second of the studies in this book, allows one on analysis to discern in how subtle a fashion and by what deviation spiritualistic rationalism has in our epoch perpetuated the spirit of those ancient fictions. One becomes aware of the way in which it still inscribes their most essential dogmas in the façade of the School. But, after having signalized that survival, it would be unjust not to state that, behind this façade, a number of original and independent minds are evolving and developing with a growing liberty and that it is the latter, who have not only very effectively contributed to the coming of a positive philosophy, but to the cultivation in the contemporary mind of the sense of relativity. In the strict domain of philosophy I should singularly weaken the value of these reflections, alter their significance and put myself in contradiction with myself, were I not to consider these, far from seeing them as adversaries, in spite of there being some restrictions as to detail with respect to some of them, as precious allies for the cause that I defend. For example, critics of knowledge such as a Poincaré, whose analyses have clarified with such a luminous light the notion of the inadequate, such as Messieurs Milhaud, Meyerson or Durkheim or moralists in the new sense of the term, such as M. Lévy Bruhl, M. Durkheim or M. Albert Bayet, a logician like M. Goblot, a promoter of the positive mind such as the author of *La Philosophie Moderne*, M. Abel Rey, to retain only a few names among so many others, who should have been cited.

When I hold as a grievance against the University the fact of its perpetuating with a rationalism that is a counterfeit of a doctrine of reason, means of persuasion of a mythological order in an epoch when means of this kind no longer have the excuse of being the only ones possible, this grievance is the more justified since, in a very great number of cases, the men whose function it is to teach the doctrines of the University are very superior to the programs that are proposed to them. It is precisely they who, in great measure. contributed to developing in minds the positive tendency, this sense of relativity, on which it will be possible to found, in substitution for rationalistic ideology, the philosophy of experience. Now, if this spiritual activity was able to formulate itself, to mark its independence in opposition to a nominal direction in a contrary sense, what a renewal could one not legitimately expect from it under the statute of a new point of view, unifying its effort, coordinating itself and substituting for an obstacle, which until now had to be skirted, the stimulus of a methodical conception?

PART I

RATIONALISM AGAINST REASON

CHAPTER ONE

THE ENCYCLOPEDIC FORMS OF RATIONALISTIC FAITH

I.—Borrowings from anterior forms of experience.

II.—Extension of the sovereignty of reason, in so far as it designates the constant part of experience, to the unstable and mobile part of experience, which relates to the moral phenomenon.

Martial, priestly, economic, according to the phases of History, there exists in every epoch and in every social group a political élite, which intends to govern man with a view to a certain interested end, one conceived with regard to itself. In no case is this egotistical finality excluded. Whether it consists in an interest in lucre and personal power, implying an exploitation, or resides in a consideration pertaining to the general interest of mankind or of a social group, it is always conceived with respect to a personal evaluation, for there is no such thing as a general interest in itself. There exist conceptions, and diverse ones, of the general interest and these conceptions are always formed in individual brains. In the hypothesis, the most distinterested one on the surface, the interest taken in the universal, wherein M. Fouillée has discerned the form of the instinct of morality, is the motive guiding the political élite. In reality, there is no disinterestedness here, but rather a transformation of egoism, and always the satisfaction of an instinct. The individuals of the élite have formed a definite conception of what is good or bad for the social

19

group or for humanity. Now, the fact that what, wrongly or rightly, they esteem as good, prevails, that constitutes for them an egotistical pleasure, just as it is one for the bookmaker for a race to be won by a horse for which he hasn't expended as much as a louis d'or. The refinement and the rarity of the egoistic motive, which, furthermore, it is extremely interesting to take into account, do not in any way change its nature.

When the opinion of the greater number assumes a great importance and becomes a force claiming obedience, the political élite is necessarily composed of men who buy a share of authority, influence and sometimes riches by willy-nilly becoming the servants of this force of the greater number. Thus it is the opinion, the will of the greater number, which is expressed by their intervention. That does not signify that this opinion, with the conception it expresses of what is good or bad for the collectivity, is to be preferred for the collectivity or even for the greater number. But what it means is that in this case, as in instances of autocracy, a constraint is exercised, that here a certain number of individual wills, instead of one alone, are established as controlling wills; these are taking over as a charge the governing of all the wills of the group and imposing upon them a rule of conduct with a view to certain ends desired by them. That signifies, in a general way, that there is a government and that there has been formed a more or less strictly determined conception of existence in common and of the ends to be aimed at.

The government has for its object to make this conception practical and to realize it in human activity and must see to its being applied not only by those giving it their spontaneous adherence, but also by those who are not followers. The means common to all political organisms with a view to such a result is to create convictions, to induce people to believe that the conception proposed by the government, the interpreter of the group's political instinct, is the best, or rather that it is the only good one, that it is *true.* Hence it is always a question of *making believe;* but the means of imposing belief differ according to the moments of civilization. Asking, at its beginnings, the required principle of suggestion of theology, the political organism now asks it of reason. Now, without inquiring here, in order to determine their value, into the different conceptions and general tendencies, which tend to impose themselves under the cover of reason, we propose to show that reason is by no means qualified to confer any authority upon these postulates and that rationalistic faith is of as fictitious a nature as theological faith itself. It will follow therefrom that all the dogmas of contemporary thought, as expressed in its political forms, would be stripped of all legitimacy if they were unable to quote another authority besides the one which they invoke for support—reason. But, again, it is not a question of sifting these dogmas themselves: by rationalistic faith we do not mean here either the actual content of this belief or the particular propositions in which it is formulated, but the fact itself that reason is held to be an ontological principle, from which rules can be drawn deductively as to the normal and social directions, that would be imposed on existence. If, finally, the intention of this study has to be underscored, we shall formulate that it does not, as it could seem, have a merely critical and negative import. Quite to the contrary. If we apply ourselves to pulling up, after the noxious theological weed, the hybrid growths that have been put forth in the shadow of the rationalistic myth, it is to make room for the harvest of experience. Without metaphor, for Reason invested with a fictitious power, we mean to substitute empiricism, the entire sum of human experience teaching the live forms of desire.

I

Theology has its share of responsibility, principally with Thomism, in the introduction of rationalism among the procedures of dialectics. It is also to this imprudent maneuver that it owes a part of its discredit. However, in order to keep this study within limits, we shall only begin with the Eighteenth Century our account of the effort with a view to conferring upon reason, set up as a dogma, an ontological value. This effort, then, shows itself to be contemporaneous with the failure of the theological fiction. For this failing fiction the political category of the social group hastens to substitute another. This new fiction is ideological in nature. The power, of which the divine person has been despoiled, is transferred to the idea and reason is regarded as the intellectual faculty, upon which the power devolves to prescribe laws in the domain of morals.

This effort was manifested in three different aspects, of which the first two, although in a milieu and by means rather different, originated in the Eighteenth Century itself and with the movement of ideas, of which the French Revolution may be taken as the most representative token and the most concrete realization. The third or last one is quite contemporary and brings into play the most subtle dialectics and the most adroit procedures in order to mask the most ingenuous ways of begging the question. The first of these aspects can be identified with the rather primary rationalism manifested in the encyclopedic doctrines, in Jacobinic dogmatism and in the naturistic conceptions of Rousseau, in which reason is sensitized under the species of instinct, according to its innate value, not yet corrupted by the social state. That is the naïve form of the rationalistic faith. It is also the one that has succeeded and become vulgarized and which, with the religion of Justice, with the religion of Truth, with the religion of Progress, with the religion of Happiness and universal Good, signify

22

to us the content of rationalistic faith. We shall examine elsewhere these different cults and penetrate the little chapels in which their faithful congregate. It will become manifest on what a narrow, contingent and mutilated interpretation of the idea of Truth and Justice the cult of these ideas reposes and what barrenness of heart or what narrowing of the intellectual field the belief implies in some, what simplicity it presupposes in others that these ideas could be realized in the domain of relation, in which the world is given us. But from this point on we are bent on searching into the question of what really constitutes rationalistic faith in this form and what positive elements it comprises, in order to aid us in our inquiry into the cause of its relative credit.

What positive elements enter into the rationalistic belief? All the anterior forms of experience, that is to say states of sensibility, instincts, products of human physiology,— states of sensibility and instincts, which, in the course of the centuries and amid the most diverse circumstances, have come into contact either to ally themselves or to combat each other, in order to acquire the right to live, to represent an hierarchical order according to the degree of strength with which they were manifested and their ability to maintain this right. And that is an infinitely embroiled and complex process, if it be considered that physiological difference, the fact of not liking the same things, naturally engenders hate and contempt among men and that, on the other hand, the similarity of appetites makes for rivalry and competition among men with a view to the possession of objects equally coveted. Thus the instincts, the estimations of the values, that have survived, having satisfied the conditions of this double trial, testify that some are resented and others accepted as right by the greater number of men composing every society of the present day. Moreover, they bear witness to the fact that, by the very existence of the society, in which they are encountered, the compromise they originated is capable of supporting the social fact. The accomplished fact, experience, militates in their favor.

There we have the most positive elements among those which form the content of rationalistic faith. There are others which, despite their including a share of chimera and mythology, are yet not to be neglected and to which one could not refuse to grant, in some degree, a positive value, if chimera and mythology are the normal means to which human mentality resorts in order to realize itself. These elements, still entering into rationalistic faith, are the very forms of the theological fiction which, for protracted periods of duration, by casting human sensibilities into one and the same mold through the imposition of a single imperative, contributed to rendering them conformable to an exemplar, which the fair play of experience had at some moment made triumphant. One must constantly have before one's eyes this consideration that, when human beings are concerned, who are endowed with the ability to imagine, the power to bovarize, that is to say to conceive things other than they are and to attribute false causalities to phenomena while ignoring the true cause, instincts are not simply imposed because they develop in the most valiant and the strongest, but also because they develop in those who are the best hypnotizers, those most capable of *making believe,* of substituting the mythological idea of truth for the fact of force, which has at some moment imposed a manner of being. This vicissitude or peripety enters into the genesis of any state of morals, of any state of belief, that has come to prevail. It has always, at some moment participated in the formation of this belief, one introduced by some sagacious representatives of a momentarily victorious state of reality. The latter, in order to spare themselves pains and by a spontaneous application of the law of the least effort,

24

profited by a momentary supremacy to catch imaginations; they acted in such a way, illustrative of the maxim of Pascal, that everything that was strong, became true. They induced belief. For constraint by violence, which had first carried the day, but whose employment would have required a constantly renewed expenditure of force, they substituted moral compulsion. Thus the peasant, who wants to defend the grains of his field against plundering birds and who yet cannot afford to immobilize his activity by remaining in the field himself, installs a scarecrow in it. In like manner the individual who wishes to avenge himself on another at little cost, threatens him by an anonymous letter with an early death from poison. Perhaps deficient in the strength to accomplish a real vengeance, he tortures the one he wishes to strike in his imagination and, if he does not actually poison his bread and his wine, he envenoms his mind. Such procedures seem base. Perhaps they are indeed, because they are frauds, means of eluding the verdicts of force, which alone generates beauty and truth; but they are essentially human, because man is endued with the power to imagine, a faculty which, although it makes his greatness, lays him open to attacks, since it is one affording enough light to give an inkling as to his sensibility, permitting it to be penetrated. The bluff, which consists in making believe that what is momentarily strong is true, eventually becomes a means of making believe that what is weak is strong. A quondam force becomes weakness continues to reign under the name of truth. That is the procedure of every ideology.

It is a procedure which one finds again in the evolution of any state of morals or manners and which plays an absolutely determinative rôle: it is the fetish and the taboo, as well as theology in all its aspects, from the humblest to the most subtle. Even if we close our eyes to the fraudulent character of this substitution to consider only the question of fact, we must surely recognize that this maneuver has a considerable influence on the formation of any social reality. For centuries the theological fiction, with the principles of persuasion it comprises, the power of constraint at its disposal, has contributed to fashioning unanimous ways of thinking, to favoring definite states of sensibility to the detriment of other states, which have been restrained and continually eliminated. It has created a state of conformism, as to ways of feeling and evaluating, among the greater number of individuals of one and the same group. It has acted like a cement made for the purpose of consolidating and fixing states of fact, which were at some moment victorious. Although, more often than not, rationalistic faith revolts against the procedures of theology, the ensemble of the articles, which for it are objects of faith, none the less draws its credibility and the sway it exercises on consciences from the long and continuous suggestion wielded by the religious fiction with respect to feelings and evaluations elaborated by empiricism, but which were at some moment withdrawn from the conflict of sensibilities by the theological bluff. Hence one must regard that slow action of theology hardening states of fact in consciences as one of the positive elements of rationalistic faith.

States of fact which have endured, states of constancy originating in experience and whose empirical derivation is easily revealed by ethnography, to these rationalistic faith, after theology, attributes an apodictical character independent of experience, a thing in itself. Under the word Reason, as it is employed by the encyclopedia or the popular sense, one discovers nothing more than empiricism sanctioned by duration and by a certain unanimity. Under the definitions given by the ideologists of Reason it is impossible to discover anything but the aleatory activities of men at grips with circumstances throughout history, and when a Michelet exclaims: "Your collective will, that is reason itself. In other words, you are gods," he is expressing with grandiloquence, with an intoxicating pathos, a cold reality, namely that there is nothing more in Reason than a relative human *parti pris* at a definite moment of history and characterized by this circumstance that, at this epoch and in this form, it is common to a great number of men. Reason, in the encyclopedic sense, is a compromise founded on a practice of variable length through duration.

What happened is this: that men, subsequent to a long stage in the course of which the play of sensibilities and of energies was adapted to collective life by theological and political compulsions, became attached to the state of sensibility, that had thus been artificially created by the encounter of instinctive impulses and social curbs. They took to be a natural product, what was the result of a compromise. They supposed that the theological and social constraints contributing to form this perfect reality, to which they had become attached, were thwarting the development of this state of sensibility; they suppressed the theological and social checks and declared that, what was the complex product of experience and of the theological fiction, was produced by Reason. That is what I have elsewhere designated as the romanticism of reason.[1]

More accurately and using a term permitting a more complete identification of the phenomenon, it is there a question of bovarysm, a complex bovarysm and one of the most ironic sort. Bovarysm, the attribution of a false causality, the fact of conceiving as engendered by an idea, an ideological thing in itself, that which results from a conflict of sensibilities, bovarysm also the fact of crystallizing in an absolute, in an immutable rule, to which man of all times can have recourse, a fluid and supple thing, whose essence is the power to modify itself in some of its features, experience; bovarysm, furthermore, the fact of

[1] See Henri Heine et le Romantisme de la Raison and La Réalité amoureuse in *La Dépendance de la Morale et L'Indépendance des Moeurs*.

regarding as contrary to the production of the phenomenon, to the expansion of rationalistic faith, the religious curb, which is one of the constitutive elements of this faith— and as a matter of fact it is from the Christian germ in its opposition to the natural instincts that are derived the conceptions of justice, liberty and equality, of which political rationalism has made a canon. These suites of interlaced bovarysms may be summarized in the nominal bovarysm, which consists in pronouncing Reason when the fact articulates Experience.

In short the rationalistic fiction proceeds after the manner of the theological fiction. A political category shows itself to be at some moment satisfied with a state of fact realized by the play of empiricism. It detaches this state of fact from the empirical roots responsible for its production and transfers it into an intangible ideological region, in which all memory of its origin is carefully abolished, where one is intent on making up a fabulous ideology for it. Like the prudent monk, who at the time of penitence spread his hands over the table-fowl and said "I baptize thee carp" the rationalist lays hold of the ever fragmentary and uncompleted bundle of human experience and says to experience: I baptize thee Reason.

Now, it is not without disadvantage to give to experience the name of reason. Interested sensibilities, political sensibilities, sensibilities of the same order as theological sensibilities of yore, the high priests of the hour exploit the legitimate dominion that experience has established over activities, to extend the benefit of this authority to decrees, of which the rigorous utility has not yet been sanctioned by experience, to rules and imperatives, whose contours the sensibilities engaged in the contentions of manners are precisely still occupied in shaping. They take the word Reason to mean more than there actually is in the word experience and thus cover certain particular tendencies, peculiar to a category, with an usurped authority. They

28

create a confusion profitable to their own conception, but this benefit is borrowed or rather stolen from the one which human activity would derive from the reality of experience, from the reality of the conflict of sensibilities among themselves concerning questions not yet decided. Rationalistic politicians declare to be resolved what is not and this anticipation is not innocuous inasmuch as it has a tendency to suppress the means whereby all reality is refined, experience.

II

But why did the political category of the nation, Eighteenth Century encyclopedists, moralistic philosophers and university pedagogues of the Nineteenth Century adopt Reason as a substitute for God? Does Reason, even made weightier by the solemnity of an annunciating capital letter, really present a reliable security and can it be said to be invested with a universal, an immutable ecumenical character? In actual fact, and especially without a capital letter, yes. But then it designates a category of definite facts, all of which refer to the conditions, under which knowledge is possible, notions of time and of space, of principles of identity and contradiction. Does it, in this aspect, differ from the rest of experience? No. According to Kant himself, at least according to a permissible interpretation of the Kantian theory of knowledge, reason is nothing else than the constant part of experience, the sum of the elements which, on analysis, one encounters in all experience, whatever, on the other hand, may be its content. Considering, without excluding any, the ensemble of the phenomena in which existence is realized, I have, for my part, taken for a dependence of this total experience the constant means, by which some fragment of existence becomes at every moment an object of knowledge for some other fragment, and these means are confounded with those which the Kantian analysis distinguished, thus becoming identified with those in which a more dogmatic interpretation sees the *a priori* immutable forms, independent of experience. These differences of appreciation are of little consequence here, for if this dogmatism of knowledge attributes to reason conceived as independent of experience an indefeasible nature and a solid certainty, metaphysical empiricism to which alone I have recourse and of which the evolutionistic empiricism of Mach is another aspect, actually attributes to it the same solidity for this precise reason that in it is considered a constant product of experience and because, in the development of experience, the rhythms in which it is expressed, determine the production of all the others. The knowledge of self is, indeed, for existence a necessity conditioning it or is, rather, implied in its essence, so that the whole of the perspectives, through which this knowledge is realized, equally assumes, once constituted, a character of necessity, which must be regarded as rigorous: any subsequent development of knowledge, which didn't place itself within this framework of knowledge, would cease being a part of the system of existence. By analogy, were one to consider the world system, it could be said of a star, which did not describe its orbit in space.

So it appears, according to either interpretation, that the term reason designates an ensemble of properties, which impose themselves in sovereign fashion on all intelligences, which are preserved from the possibility of being altered by any schism, while at the same time these properties refer to definite functions, which themselves relate to a necessity of knowledge. To confine ourselves to a definition of reason formulated in purely empirical terms, it will be denominated the part of experience, which is invariably repeated like itself, the rigid and fixed portion of it, which could not be modified without jeopardizing the phenomenon of existence, such as it appears and represents itself to our mind. One

30

will say it is that in contradistinction to the part of experience, which, through these fixed cadres that it constitutes, improvises itself, diversifies itself and brings to existence the portion of the unforeseen and of change, by which it escapes an absolute systematization.

Consequently one understands the interest prompting new moralists to bring about this nominal bovarysm, by which they try to deceive themselves. To define their maneuver in the light, in which it most clearly reveals its game, to kindle the lights in this place where the moral interest maintains an obscurity propitious to phantoms, it appears that they lay hold of the word reason, which denotes the fixed rhythms of experience, its immutable part, to apply it to the mobile part of experience, to its portion that is in the process of constant improvisation and which is more especially expressed in the moral phenomenon. They strive, in a word, by an illegitimate extension of the word reason, to make the uncertain and undetermined part of experience benefit from the prestige of infallibility rightly enjoyed by the part of experience, which has become solid as a means of knowledge. They give the name of what is fixed, of what is above discussion, to what is fluid, to what at every current moment is in question. Rationalistic faith, however paradoxical that may seem, is expressed in the fact of covering the irrational with the cloak of reason. The aim of this maneuver, as we have already divulged, is to make believe, to the benefit of a personal valuation, that what is in question is resolved—to use a metaphor, to make believe that the battle has been won in order to elude an attack.

How can so paradoxical an undertaking be successful, even were it in an incomplete fashion? We have tried to explain it by showing that, in the moral domain, certain principles developed in the course of one and the same civilization by a relatively constant experience and by theological constraints have become crystallized in automatic tendencies. Another consideration is also of a nature to explain the phenomenon. It relates to the representation formed in one's mind of the development of experience, to the deep-rooted conception, of theological origin, according to which existence, governed by the virtuality of a first cause, would evolve from a first beginning toward an intentional and logical end by a series of rigorous deductions. In the light of this representation reason, in consideration of the fixity of its action, is held to be this first cause. The logical principles, which it stipulates and in which it entirely consists, are considered the first manifestation of its development and what, in moral experience, at some given moment presents some appearance of universality is regarded as a consequence of that first development of these logical principles.

This representation, need it be said, is formed in violation of the principle of causality, whose play governs our mentality and destroys as an obstacle to its functioning any hypothesis of a first cause. As soon as one makes of the laws of the mind the logical use they prescribe, it is seen to be contrary to an entirely different conception, the following one: the intuitions, the principles of reason are, in the development of experience, creations of experience, rhythms which are repeated indefinitely like themselves and through which passes, in conformity with the exigencies of causality, the flux without beginning or end of experience. In such a representation the rôle attributed to reason is that of a frame through which all the rest of experience elapses, the latter conserving the mystery of its indiscernible genesis, whereas, in the representation evoked by rationalistic belief, the rôle of reason is that of a source, of a source which, against all likelihood, would not owe its formation to any antecedent water and whose outflow would, in progressing, engender all the forms and all the transitory aspects of the world to settle, stagnant, in one knows not what basin with definite contours.

Rationalistic faith, then, reposes, we repeat, on a fraud. This fraud is practised to the advantage of morality, in which is expressed, in its most intense form, the human will for power. Moved by this will for power every individual sensibility, in whatever aspect it may be manifested, wishes to make of its particular desire the law of the universe. How does one go about realizing this metamorphosis? By throwing oneself into the medley and by persuasion, by example and by violence, imposing one's conception of wɪɪ t ought to be, by acting in such a way that what one wishes becomes what is, what will be. Most certainly, but the attempt is hazardous. Then one must persuade oneself and others that, what is the wish of one individual sensibility is the expression of an already preexistent law, that what it is a question of creating is already created, that what has to be improvised and imposed by armed force, has existed from time immemorial and can be deduced. This is the precise bovarysm of morality, which forthwith resorts to the bovarysm of false causality: for the genuine determinism of morality, the conflict of the sensibilities, one substitutes a false determinism, a pure idea, *causa sui*. To morality one ascribes Reason as its origin. To reason, which governs experience in its logical forms, because it is in this respect the transfer of a prior experience, one constantly repeating itself identical to itself, it attributes the power to govern experience in its most unstable forms, under that form of tastes and colors, the contention of which makes all the fluid part of life and withdraws it from mechanism.

CHAPTER TWO

THE KANTIAN FORMS OF RATIONALISTIC FAITH

I.—Extension of the sovereignty of reason, in so far as it designates the forms of knowledge, to the domain in which it would apply to the forms of action.
II.—The illegitimate character of this extension. What, amid the perspectives opened by the forms of knowledge, would be the veritable form of action?

I   1817290

Whereas encyclopedic rationalism expresses the rationalistic belief in its popular forms, as it were, and in so far as it affirms itself without being concerned with a demonstration, Kantism interprets this same belief in its learned forms and, moreover, in an artificial milieu and one that is no more qualified to engender a true belief than professors and scholars are to form a language. Just like a language a faith arises spontaneously and is not something that one consciously fabricates. In this artificial form the rationalistic belief undergoes the fate of religious faith, which prepares its ruin as soon as it appeals to reasoning in order to prove itself.

What is Reason in the Kantian sense? Without doubt this term, when Kant began to speculate, denoted for him intelligence as a whole, our faculty of knowing. In the first Kantian sense reason refers essentially to knowing as opposed to being, to activity, which develops in the universe and to which knowing applies. What are the relationships of knowing and being? In what measure can we accept as correct the pieces of information, which knowing brings us on being and on action, the information of the subject on the object? And Kant, soon tending toward an interpretation which is going to distinguish reason, as to its very nature and its essence from the other elements of intelligence, wonders if there do not exist kinds of knowledge or perceptions of truth which experience cannot explain and of which it can, therefore, be said that they do not derive from experience. This, in my opinion, is posing the question wrongly and comprehending under the term experience an incomplete and truncated notion of genuine experience. Such a confusion comes from the categorical and realistic character attributed by Kant to the opposition of being and knowing, from the impervious partitions he sets up between these two notions, from that arbitrary dualism, which will prevent him, throughout his speculative career, from relating to the idealistic monism, in which Berkeley had already found a more coherent interpretation of the metaphysical fact.

If it is, indeed, permissible to dissociate the idea of knowledge from the idea of existence, one must not forget that such a dissociation can only be made from a point of view created in the mind by the very development of the fact of existence, that the relationship, which has been established between knowing and being, itself belongs, by virtue of dependence, to the general process of existence, that it is made of experience. There remains that, from this broader point of view, one can wonder, after the fashion of Kant, whether, in the rapport created by this experimental process of a metaphysical nature, there do not exist certain constant, universal rhythms, which are therefore common to any conceivable experience. Then we shall not say that these rhythms are independent of experience, but establish contrariwise that they compose its skeleton, that upon which afterwards all the ensuing facts, in which experience is diversified, are inserted.

If Kant, moreover, by some dogmatism in the expression, was able to induce the belief that he meant to designate by the forms of knowledge something extraneous to experience, the procedures he uses to discover its forms attest, on the contrary, that the latter are identified with what is constant in experience and such was doubtless, as we have already noted, his first manner of seeing things. It is in this sense that M. Hoeffding interpreted his method. "One discovers forms," he says, "by observing what is constant in our knowledge, whereas matter is what is susceptible to changing and variation. . . ."[1] Now, what is our knowledge thus taken as an object of observation for itself, if it is not experience itself? As I enounced it in *Les Raisons de l'Idealisme,* it is necessary and sufficient for knowledge, such as it is given us, to be possible, that there exist in the mind invariable rhythms always repeating themselves, in terms of which other unstable and perpetually changing rhythms are assembled in a suite of representations having a common bond among them. This second series is no less necessary than the first to constitute the fact of knowledge, nor is the first less indispensable than the second; but we do not relinquish given experience to attain either one, which do not differ among themselves except by the constancy manifested by some and the whimsical multiplicity, which characterizes the others. This established and which permits one, with Hume's viewpoint alone, to construct the system of knowledge upon which Kant ventures, there is nothing to prevent naming, with Kant, forms of knowledge whatever is constant in what is given of the fact of experience and matter of knowledge whatever, in this datum is variable. One will likewise agree to entitle more especially reason the ensemble of the forms of knowl-

[1] *Histoire de la Philosophie Moderne,* Alcan, p. 49.

edge, which are subject to constant rhythms. Reason will then be the ensemble of the propositions derived from intuition as well as from the understanding, in the Kantian sense of these two terms, the ensemble of those propositions, on which human sensibilities and intelligencies agree and which form the guiding-marks, in relation to which all the rest is evaluated, in terms of which reality is perceived by men in the same light, in terms of which science is constituted. . . . It is that through which all the diverse is perceived and conceived, all the diverse, which is the matter to which, in order to compare its manifestations on one and the same plane, the synthetic activity of the mind is applied. It is thus that all things are given us in time, in space, in causal succession, in quantity and in quality.

When the word reason is restricted to signifying only these positive notions, it has for the human mind the most precious value of all. That is the scientific meaning of the word, by which it denotes the power of the intellect over things and that a common plan has been formed, amid the perspectives of being, according to which the most diverse things enter into relation and comparison with one another, constituting with all their differences a universe. But, after having given this positive description of reason, after having inspired confidence in its virtue, in its character of universality and of common intelligibility in the limited field of the forms of knowledge, Kant, utilizing this distinct nature, independent of experience, which he also attributed to it, executes the same maneuver as the popular and naïve rationalism which has been the question at issue. For this restricted field of the forms of knowledge, in which reason exercises a sovereign authority, he substitutes the field of action, in which experience improvises itself freely and independently and to this reason which he has just so rigorously defined, all of whose power is exhausted after it has fixed the movements of experience in action on the common plane of knowledge, he at-

38

tributes the new power, totally foreign to the properties with which he has endued it, to decide, among the diversity of the modes in which action is manifested, which are legitimate and which illicit. Under the name of a faculty, whose function it is to make objects of knowledge of the modes of action, he introduces a myth, which would have the entirely different power of imposing rules on action, of decreeing its law. The ambiguity in which, as has been shown, the vulgar philosophical sense had let itself get caught, is again performing its office. This sophistry, however, is singularly crass and the fact of its having been accepted by minds used to dialectical methods betokens that the moral appetite created by anterior disciplines maintains an extraordinary critical deafness; that also attests to the pusillanimous fear under the sway of which one seems to believe, in political milieus or sets, whose mentality is more or less faithfully reflected in universities, that, *the former means of morality being ruined, there is no morality possible.*

Kant, we know, pretended to discover practical reason by the same analytical procedures he had used to discover theoretical reason. As he had distinguished between the form and the matter of knowledge, he pretended to distinguish between the form and the matter of action, and he imagined that he could elevate into the metaphysical palace he was constructing, like two symmetrical wings, these two distinctions, of which one was made in the heart of knowledge and the other in the heart of action. But such a pretension is based on that extraordinary blindness, of which it can be said that only the power of moral prejudice explains that it was possible for it to be shared by other philosophers and that it has not until now been exposed by criticism. That blindness consists in not seeing that action is itself implicit in this matter, in this content of knowledge, which Kant distinguishes from its form, so that being a part of the whole that he is considering, knowledge, it cannot be symmetrically opposed to this whole, which embraces it. The action of the human person, the action called voluntary, is a fragment of this matter making up the content of knowledge, which is expressly its object. It appears through the same perspectives of space, time, causality through which all other objects appear. It is one of the objects, to which the forms of theoretical reason apply. Hence there is no ground for seeking a form of action, were it human action, as one was searching out a form of knowledge; or at least these two categories of research cannot be opposed to each other as facts of the same importance, inasmuch as one is implied in the other, being a subdivision thereof. Human actions, voluntary actions can only, we must repeat, appear among the traced cadres and perspectives described by Kant for all the other objects of experience. The action called voluntary belongs to the world of experience like the chemical property or like the development of the plant.

II

If, after this verification, it is still a question of applying to this fragment of total experience the process of distinction, that was applied by Kant to the total experience itself, if one wishes, in the particular fact of knowledge which voluntary action is, to distinguish form from matter, as was done with respect to the fact of knowledge itself in its generality, there remains that in it one must bring into relief, just that and nothing more, what is common to every voluntary action, that without which no voluntary action is conceivable, in order to have the form of the action consist of it. Moreover, in everything that differs, in everything that is not constant, one must recognize matter, the content of the action. Now, one can say that action reputed to be voluntary is recognized straightaway by this that the one, who accomplishes it and the one conscious of it is single, one and the same agent. This in fact is common to any voluntary action, this is truly a universal property of voluntary action which permits one to distinguish it from all other actions that are manifested in nature—from electrical action, from the action of weight, from the action of light and of heat. Here we really have a *form* of action. The distinction is founded to this point that the mind grants, according to cases, two different meanings to the same term action and that in pronouncing the same word to designate, for example, a short-circuit which has caused an accident involving persons or a theft committed by a burglar, each is fully cognizant of employing one and the same word in two different senses. If it were a matter of defining the nuance existing between the two terms, one would have no other means, without prejudging some metaphysical or moral question, that of the personality or that of liberty, than to resort to the distinction, which has just been indicated, and to say that in one case the action emanates from a force that is not sensible of its manifestation and its effects; in the other it emanates from a force that is also conscious of the activity in which it expresses itself.

Confusion in one and the same center of the energy, which produces the action, and of the energy taking cognizance of it, here then is the form of voluntary action and particularly of human action. It is this form, which was already elucidated in *La Dependance de la Morale et l'Independance des Moeurs,* yet in that work there was superimposed on the pure and simple fact of consciousness here invoked a fact of valuation, a judgment made on the act by the agent who performs it, a judgment qualifying the act good or bad. By that addition we arrived more directly, beyond human action, which can at times be instinctive or even purely reflex, at properly moral action such as Kant especially kept in view. The form of the moral action was situated in a fact of non-indifference on the part

41

of the agent with respect to the act he performed.[1] We noted, in order to establish it more clearly, by way of distinction, that the moral act is the product a double causal series, one determining the act and the other determining estimation.

Such a definition of the form of moral action is strictly consonant with the method employed by Kant to determine the form of knowledge. It is rich in consequences. It authorizes certain general propositions, certain deductions of the nature of those presented by geometry or logic, the latter, for example, which could give rise to numerous corollaries and bring about many an application: *When the two causal series, which intervene in the production of the moral action result in stipulating the same act, a psychological state is produced, which is called "good conscience"; when these two causal series command a different act, a psychological state is produced that is called "bad conscience."*

Finally, beyond the deductive science, which this proposition can found, the formal angle, that we have traced, opens on the multiplicity of moral experience, which is expressed in human conduct, in the modes of sensibility while following the variations of circumstances of time and place, in terms of the social fact and the degree of scientific knowledge, and that is matter, all the matter of action.

With respect to this matter of action, knowledge is exercised like a science of observation in the same way as it is practised in regard to the different bodies, whose chemical composition or physical modalities it distinguishes. Now, it is precisely for this attitude of observation, which permits one to derive certain laws, certain constant ways of being of bodies and to exploit nature while obeying it, it is for this attitude of observation that the critique of practical reason substituted an imperative attitude: the gesture

[1] *La Dépendance de la Morale et l'Indépendance des Moeurs,* Société du Mercure de France, pp. 62-69.

of the decree. Having eluded the necessity of making the form of action inhere in what is common to any action, as it had made the form of knowledge inhere in what is common to any fact of knowledge, critical philosophy nevertheless pretended to subject the live source, the entirely irrational principle, from which the diverse modes of action rise to a command provided with a character of universality. To proceed in this manner was precisely, to come to the point of specifying this character of universality, to begin by retrenching the elements, which alone could constitute it. Hence the principle of Kantism—of a form of individual action such that it may become a general law for all men—is entirely empty. It consecrates the backwards or wrong way philosophy, since individual action, moral action, with the creations it realizes in the order of sensibility, is precisely the element destined to introduce into the phenomenal drama the portion of diversity, of difference which animates it and distinguishes it from mechanism.

What is happening? It is that so empty a principle is only filled with some content to the extent that a particular instinct establishes itself in it and, under the disguise of a general formula, endeavors to prevail. In this light the rationalism of practical reason shows itself to be what it is in reality and for the same reason as encyclopedic rationalism: an episode of the struggle of instincts with the purpose of dominating. It is, to speak the language of Carlyle, an episode of vulpine nature. It is a question, for some particular instinct, of seizing upon the empty formula of Kantism and establishing itself in it. With it it will ennoble itself, it will don the buskin, will deceive with a higher, more imposing exterior. It is its voice, its voice of some particular instinct, articulated and sonorous emitted by the organs of some living and concrete individual, which will attribute its form and its destiny to the universal; but this voice will make itself heard like that of the chanter in church, from the height of a tribune, according to an acoustics wittingly prepared, which will multiply its volume.

It is, let us note, in the light of the beautiful Kantian experimental method instituting a distinction between the form and the content of knowledge, that the critique of practical reason shows its entirely unreasonable character and attests to the most flagrant violation of the method it invokes. It is for having carefully neglected to distinguish the veritable and patent form from the practise that it was possible to present as a form a mask, under which is hidden the will to power of an instinct. This instinct is the Christian instinct, which it will be easy to identify when one makes an inventory of the states of sensibility, which make up the content of rationalistic faith.

Such is the second aspect of this faith, its dialectical aspect. Under this form, as under the preceding one, its aim is to introduce, to the profit of a particular state of sensibility, an intellectual principle of certitude in a domain, in which the conflict of sensibilities alone decides at every moment as to the state of morals, which should reign. Only so immediate an interest explains the credit, with minds inured to analysis, of so chimerical a proposition, and the thesis of a form of the application resulting in a logical imperative can be regarded as one of the most extraordinary, to which moral bias, in its social aspect, has given rise.

Chapter Three

THE PEDAGOGICAL FORMS
OF THE RATIONALISTIC BELIEF

I.—How one makes up a rational genealogy for reason.

II.—A description of reason with a view to distinguishing it from other activities of the mind produced in its name. The moral and scientific modalities of psychological activity.

I

As a matter of fact this aspect of the rationalistic belief is already an historical aspect. The most recent moralists use other expedients to have the moral principles, which they deem useful, consecrated by reason and to persuade themselves that morality, which is a fact, is a principle.

If, instead of saying the most recent *rationalists,* I say the most recent *moralists,* it is because rationalism, in its mystical form, consists—we have just seen it on the occasion of the two preceding forms of the rationalistic belief —in applying the principles of reason to categories of facts, which precisely do not depend on reason, and because it is actually in the domain of morality that this unseasonable use of reason is practised with the greatest rigour. Just as with its present-day representatives, so with the previous ones, rationalism allows its tendentious character to be divined. It is always a question of *making believe* that a way of feeling, of thinking, of evaluating, which conflicts with others and whose more or less keen fascination is in short its only legitimate title, draws its validity not from its force, but from its truth; it is always a matter of persuading that what depends on the category of conflict, depends on the logical category. For the contemporary protagonists of rationalistic faith, as for the preceding ones, what is involved is founding morality on reason. It is a question, by attributing this solid foundation to it, of making a transmissible notion of it, an object of teaching. More openly, more consciously than in prior epochs, this concern of teaching is at the base of all the endeavors made to rationalize morality and it is, moreover, in the world of teaching that all these attempts came into being. Since, more often than not, they emanate from very perspicacious minds, reason is not introduced into them immediately and directly, as it was in the course of the previous forms of faith. It is no longer invoked but *a posteriori,* in the quality of a consecration and most often, strictly speaking, it is not brought in any more except in an entirely nominal and artificial manner. By a dialectic borrowed from other intellectual means one gets the proof required by the moral thesis established and, furthermore, whatever the value of this proof may be, the designation of rational is always applied to it. Thus reason is introduced into the affair in order that it may lend the support and the prestige of its name to the moral imperatives, which are to be propagated. It then becomes the substitute for the most diverse realities or intellectual fictions; it signifies everything but reason in the legitimate sense of the term, but its name punctuates all periods. And that is like a disease of the philosophical mind, like a neurosis of the logical faculty of the nature of the verbal tic constraining certain individuals to keep intercalating into the fabric of their discourse a word that is always the same and which has no bearing on the object of their logical thought.

Unless, in this incoherent recall, one must see the final

term of an evolution, the one in which things destined to disappear still, by an unavailing presence, recall a former utility. This word reason, with nothing in it any more but what is foreign to itself, would in the theses of philosophers and sociologists no longer be anything but a testimonial organ, a last vestige of an evolution of morality, but which no longer has even ornamental value, which breaks the line of dialectical construction and weakens some theses which, without this recourse, would not be destitute of value.

How, under such conditions, does the use of the word still contrive to delude? More often than not by the absence of any definition, which permits its use now in one sense and now in very different meanings. Sometimes, in the course of grave treatises, the illusion is produced by another procedure. By means of a scrupulously correct definition formulated in the chapter treating of reason one gains the reader's ~~confidence,~~ or perhaps even one's own confidence. This credit allows one afterwards, in the chapter in which one treats of morality, to introduce incidentally, equipped with a new signification, under which it was not understood in the first definition, this reason whose support one wishes to secure at any price. If the reader's mind is not immediately on guard, if it accepts the covert suggestion, an ambiguity is created, from which the moral theme will unscrupulously profit. Now, in the environments where this theme is produced under its philosophical forms, milieus predisposed to accept it by heredity, by education and also by virtue of considerations of professional or social interest, the insinuation is more often than not and easily accepted. In these milieus it is the same as in those salons of the demi-monde presented by one of our novelists, in which sonorous appellations are *de rigueur*, where the most plebeian names enhance themselves with unexpected particles, where, by the unctuous voice of the maitre d'hôtel taking the place of patents, each visitor is promoted, willy-nilly, to baron, viscount or marquis at the hazard of euphony, while these titles said again and again insistently by the hosts of the place find themselves confirmed by the accessory acquiescence of all. The milieus, in which morality is fabricated under the cover of philosophy, do not show more scruple, nor are they welcomed less eagerly and the theses, which are produced there under the auspices of reason find the authenticity of the titles, with which they adorn themselves, only little contested. However, just as the false personages of the outskirts of society could not deceive those, who know the true ones, there is no better means of avoiding becoming a dupe of moral theses, in which reason is falsely invoked, than to have constantly before the mind a definition, a precise concept of what reason is in reality.

II

This definition was previously given, when we intimated that it is the part of experience, which is invariably repeated like itself according to constant rhythms, as opposed to that other part of experience which, in the common framework of these constant rhythms, improvises itself and diversifies itself, bringing to existence the portion of the unforeseen and of change, by which it escapes an absolute systematization. From a viewpoint of pure logic it will be equally possible to define reason as follows: the ensemble of the invariable circumstances, with which no affirmation of the mind can engage in contradiction without denying itself in so far as possible.

Reason is this and nothing more. When reason, then, is invoked to designate some activity differing from the one just described, this will be the sign that one is announcing, in its name, another allegorical personage.

If reason in its principle is an activity, it is indeed a

strictly defined activity. In practice it is utilizable only as an activity of control and supervision. What identifies it, and on this one could not insist too much, is the character of repetition of the movement in which it expresses itself, by which, constantly on the alert, it opposes the introduction into experience of any movement of a nature to thwart its own. It is a repetition of the *same* and incessantly reproduces the same gestures; it never improvises. By this continuous movement of repetition it keeps constantly open the cadres of duration and of space, among which phenomena will have to be manifested in order to form a part of one universe; it stipulates the condition of non-contradiction, to which these phenomena will be held to conform in order to figure in the cosmic drama. This is considerable, and it is nothing. It is considerable, for, without the intervention of this gesture of constant repetition, the spectacle would have no unity. It is nothing in this sense that, were everything limited to this fact of repetition, the scene of the universe would remain empty. Now, this scene is not empty; it is pervaded with a prodigiously varied improvisation, in the course of which a multitude of phenomena, all satisfying the conditions specified by the play of reason, combine or clash together. Now, with these phenomena it is still a question of an activity, and it is on the encounter of this activity with that of reason that the ambiguity ably maintained by the rationalistic philosophers of the most modern mode is based. This equivocation begins when, in everyone's language or in that of these philosophers, these new phenomena are designated as *reasonable* activity, inasmuch as they are declared to be engendered by a reasonable activity from the mere fact of not engaging in any opposition to any of the exigencies stipulated by the movements of reason. Now, to define them by this fact of non-opposition is not defining them at all and amounts to saying nothing of them, since they wouldn't be anything without submitting to this condition. Consequently there remains the need to define this activity by positive characteristics, if one wishes to be able to distinguish and recognize it, and, in lieu of enouncing that it is a reasonable activity, which is speaking without saying anything, one must on the contrary differentiate it from the activity of reason by exposing that it is precisely what is added to this activity in order to permeate its empty cadres. So that ambiguity may be avoided, it will be necessary to banish this term of reasonable activity, which provides us with no information about the object it designates and, contrary to a genuine definition, serves only to maintain a confusion.

Every activity that is produced in the universe is, we insist, produced in it conformably to the principles of reason and satisfies the conditions of space, duration and determinism stipulated by them. An activity which did not conform to these principles taken in the strict sense they express, would not be a part of the universe on which we are speculating. But, in the measure in which it adds something to this primordial play of the peculiar activity of reason, the activity, which develops in the play of existence, merits the name of empirical activity; what interests us, for the precise data we seek to attain, is to discern what this activity brings that is peculiar to itself, apart from the circumstance according to which it conforms to the principles of reason. Now, this search reveals a very rich harvest of diverse elements. Is it a question of the inanimate world? To this activity must be attributed the infinite variety of chemical properties, in which the peculiarities of matter are manifested, the physical laws, in which are inscribed the relations engendered among all the modalities by the determinism of force. Is it a question of the organic world? We are still dealing with the same principle. Moreover, confounded with these properties and these first laws, the sensations, in terms of which these laws and these properties exist and which are their subjective aspect.

Then there are the instincts, in which these properties and these laws continue to act and are most closely combined with sensation, mother of the fact of consciousness. Is it finally a question of the mental world? A more minute discrimination imposes itself on criticism, for it is on the occasion of this category of action that rationalistic sophism tries to insinuate its ambiguity. Now, what does the mental introduce into the world of phenomena? On one hand intentions, aims, a finality. Thereby the mental shows its point of suture with the world of the instincts, for it is instinct that hatches desire, in following the variations of which teleology appears. An appearance of the most potent interest. It is intentional activity, brought forth by the arbitrary improvisations of chemisms and of instincts, which introduces on the stage of the universe the intrigue, in which existence becomes impassioned and shows itself to be worthy to be lived. Now, in this improvisation of instinct and taste instituting finalities, there is no intervention of the activity of reason: provided that the creations of taste and instinct, with the finalities they command, are inscribed in the cadres of space and time, whatever, moreover, they may be and as entirely arbitrary as they, on the other hand, aver themselves to be—here they are in conformity with the activity of reason. It is only the habit we have of our desires and of the ends they pursue, which prevents our seeing what they have in themselves independently of any necessity.

Thus the mental introduces, on the one hand, intentions and ends into the world of phenomena and we have brought out that the activity of reason is wholly expended by the mere fact that it allowed these intentions and these ends to be introduced on the common plane of the universe, as not counteracting any of the immutable rhythms, in which it expresses itself; we emphasized that it has no quality to decide after that as to their respective value. The mental introduces besides on this same stage of the world, and

51

in terms of the finality it stipulates, another category of elements, another category of activity with reflection having this finality in view. Now, this thoughtful activity, which, in its most perfect forms, engenders scientific activity has nothing in common either with the activity of reason. If reason is not the agent which invents or indicates an end to attain, neither is it the agent, which, after the end to be attained has been fixed by desire, searches for or invents the proper means to gain this now determined end. This appropriate action is produced or not produced, contingent upon the wealth or the poverty of invention, which has nothing to do with the activity of reason. Only in its relationship with this new mode of activity does it reveal that it is always and everywhere what it shows itself to be. It stipulates, with the cadres which it never ceases to open and to present to any attempt at improvisation, the ensemble of the conditions to which that improvisation has to submit in order to be a part of universal experience.

Finally, reason isn't the agent either, which resolves to submit means to the control of reflection, for deciding this still forms, in the bosom of mental activity, a spontaneous decision, which can be made or not be made by virtue of a psychological disposition, one that has nothing in common with reason. The act could be impulsive and it might happen that in these conditions the agent improvised a series of means perfectly adapted in fact to the end to be attained. Experience alone would make known whether the means employed are or are not adapted to this end, real experience, that is to say the success or the failure of the undertaking. Now, in this case one could not say that the activity, which would here have been displayed, was of a rational nature; it would only be a question there of an aleatory activity fortuitously found to be compatible with the modes of reality, and which could just as well not have accorded with them. But man is gifted with the power to imagine and to represent to himself in certain cases and in a certain measure the consequences and the repercussions of his acts prior to accomplishing them. That supposes the memory of a past experience with the ability to repeat it and to forecast it in one's mind with the consequences, with which one knows it to be fraught. Such a power permits man to replace real experience with the projected image of reality, thus economizing his activity and enabling him to choose among different acts, imagined and tested like a blank cartridge, as it were, the one which will have the best chances, in the course of its effort toward an intentional aim, not to clash with any of the angles of reality. Such an activity, which discovers means permitting the attainment of an end, calls into play faculties of inhibition, faculties of imagination and a power of anticipation; nevertheless it is not reason. It exists in people in very diverse degrees, being exercised with greater or lesser success. Either accompanied or not by anticipatory images, more or less impulsive, more or less reflective, the trials brought forth by this activity will only be judged by the event. At the most one can say, after the event has decided, that it will have disclosed with respect to the abortive endeavors a contradiction between their elements and the conditions of the possible, and that reason has intervened here under the form of the principle of contradiction in order to exclude these unfortunate attempts from reality. Saying as much will have the effect of marking better the difference between two kinds of activity: the one that has invented the attempt and the one which eventually intervenes to bring the principle of contradiction into play. The latter, the activity of reason, will be manifested in the form of this activity of control, which has been attributed to it and which is evinced by the incessant and invariable repetition of the same movements. As for the other activity, after it has been ascertained that, under its improvising or reflective forms, it is independent of reason, it will remain to call attention to the fact that it is itself active with very diverse consequences, according to whether it is a question of science or of morality.

Science is the inquiry into what are the modes of reality in a domain, in which these modes have been formulated independently of the activity that searches into them. Morality is the inquiry into the question of what the modes of reality should be in a domain, where the activity searching into these modes is the very one which engenders them and must engender them before they can become objects of science.

Science confines itself to formulating what is and its formulas offer very different degrees of generality and, depending on the orders of facts it is considering, open up a field of application of a more or less vast extent. Purely deductive in the measure in which, with geometry, logic or mathematics, it studies the modes of those gestures of constant repetition, which relate to the form of reason, it promulgates laws, which enjoy the same character of universality shown by the constant part of experience, to which it applies. Having then recourse to observation and noting, among the inflexible cadres determined by the first inquiry, facts of empirical improvisation such as the properties of the diverse bodies of matter, which could not be deduced from the previously established laws, it may be said to enter another realm. Science in this new domain offers a character of application all the more general, because the facts it observes are themselves repeated with more constancy, are fixed in a more definitive fashion and are more independent of the movement of evolution and of metamorphosis, which is pursued amid the play of phenomena. Besides, whatever may be the phenomena upon which it bears, science never applies to any but those among them, which belong, in the general order of evolution, to *the category of what has become.*

Here one may place the limit, which expressly distinguishes it from moral activity. The latter refers to phenomena of which some, the more general ones, if one consults experience, indeed show a certain degree of fixity, but the greater number of which are in process of formation and receive varied and unstable solutions from the diversity of sensibilities.

Phenomenal genesis, such as it was described in *Les Raisons de l'Idealisme,* supposes that every phenomenal series being formed in the course of this genesis necescessarily appears in the schemes opened by the series immediately anterior to it. This condition imposes itself because, without it, this new series would not be a part of the universe on which we are speculating. Such a viewpoint, then, supposes that this new series will depend on the antecedent determinism; but it in no wise supposes that before its appearance it can be scientifically determined, for, if it must, with the different phenomena constituting it, take its place within cadres previously traced, it can reveal itself in them under the most diverse aspects. In terms of causality one could say, by way of explanation, that the cause here is of much wider extent than the reality which will proceed from it. Therefore the power of improvisation operating in existence retains every latitude to exert itself amid those perspectives. Such is the case in whatever relates to morality, in which this power of improvisation operating in existence develops, under the species of our own activity, the uncertain modes of the future.

Moral activity could, therefore, under no pretext, be comprised in the category of scientific activity. One must even question if it belongs to reflective activity. In fact, unless one appeals to Platonic ideologism, if one refuses to imagine a world of ideas, by which the world of experience would have to be guided, the moral fact, by the place it occupies in the extreme point of the development of existence, must be considered, in its essentials, an empirical invention of sensibility fixing the valuations good and evil on the modes of action and not the search for a norm already in existence. It is from this viewpoint that, in *La Dépendance de la Morale et l'Indépendance des Moeurs,* in opposition to the dialectical category on which phenomena depend, which become the subject of the grasp of science and computation, we instituted a category of conflict in which to situate the moral phenomenon, that is to say an evaluation stressing the invention of sensibility in following the variations of which it becomes clear that this could hold its legitimacy only from the authority and the force with which those promulgating it, as a personal manner of being, are able to impose it.

If, however, a fact of invention of this nature is essential to the genesis of the moral phenomenon, being the condition *sine qua non* of its production, one can still admit, from the fact of its being produced in an agent capable of reflection, that certain objective considerations will contribute to the composition of its definitive aspect, under which it will come into being in the world of phenomena, in the closed field in which it is called to struggle. One can, for example, grant that the agent will take into account the difficulties, which would oppose its realization from the fact of other valuations already formulated by his own sensibility or strongly represented in the social environment. It may be conceded that, under the sway of these considerations, the moral fact will be modified to some extent, but, apart from the fact that these considerations already pertain to the domain of conflict—being forms of the apprehension caused by the prospect of conflict—one must recognize, after that, that thus modified the new moral evaluation will still owe its legitimacy only to the outcome of a conflict, whose terms are aleatory, notably the degree of power of the creative sensibility itself, the degree of power of the agent, the exactitude of the calculation accomplished by the agent with a view to the more or less important modifications to be undergone by the fact of sensibility and the degree of opposition of the environment.

Hence there remains, if it is possible to assign a part to reflective activity in the domain of moral phenomena, that this part does no more than add, so to speak, a new element of chance to an order of facts, whose genesis is immersed in pure empiricism. Any attempt to demonstrate its validity dialectically is destitute of signification, or is only a mask to dissimulate the struggle of a sensibility, which is striving to dominate another with it. There remains that, with the moral fact, one is in the realm of life *which is becoming,* in the domain of struggle for existence and for the occupation of the ground among diverse species of sensibility, which are what they are and among which the one destined to prevail will establish only in the sequel, according to the transcript of its valuations, the rules of good and evil.

No mode of activity, then, is more removed from the firm activity of reason than this precarious moral activity, subject to variation at the will of sensibilities, which prevail by turns in a human group in the bosom of one and the same civilization or amongst successive civilizations. Now, the aim of the rationalists of the pedagogical period, as it was that of the encyclopedic or Kantian rationalists, is to place under the dependence of reason this moral activity, which offers the most striking contrast with the characteristic forms of reason.

CHAPTER FOUR

THE METAMORPHOSES OF REASON IN THE TEACHING OF MORALITY

I

We already noted that the procedure of moralists consists in appealing, in order to demonstrate morality, to a class of considerations extraneous to reason and then, when this demonstration seems to them to have been completed, abruptly invoking the authority of reason in its behalf with the aim of attributing an indisputable character to their thesis, one which is able, by the intimidation of the name, to vanquish all forms of resistance.

Such an assertion could, however, seem unwarranted if we did not show by some examples that moralists of the best repute do not employ any different means and that their skill alone, more often than not favored by the prestige of the professor, manages to conceal the simplicity of the stratagem from benevolent consciences. This ability is sometimes displayed, as we said, in the reserve and the propriety they evince when treating separately with the principles of reason, and this reserve and this propriety, we added, have the effect of creating a disposition favorable to confidence and a critical blindness, which will, at the right time, permit the introduction, without awakening suspicion, of propositions the furthest removed from this first version.

This is the case, for instance, with M. Malapert and in the case of M. Malapert, as in some other examples of professors of philosophy, whose names and examples will be invoked here, as in those in our lycées and secondary schools using analogous procedures, I am far from suspecting the good faith of the thinker. Where they are concerned I confine myself to the hypothesis, according to which the philosopher deceives himself by an unconscious maneuver, before imposing on his listeners or his readers. I shall limit myself to this hypothesis save for welcoming the tacit protest of those—there is more than one at the present time—who, solicitous above all about the integrity of their thought, have established tight partitions between their teaching, consonant with the programs, and their own philosophical reflection.

If, moreover, M. Malapert is implicated here, it is because his *Leçons de Philosophie* is one of the works in which, by reason of great qualities of exposition, the classical teaching of these last years frequently seeks its directions. Now, if one consults these lessons in the chapter dealing with rational principles, one ascertains that the author classes among these principles only the principle of identity and the principle of causality, which he regards as the only legitimate forms of the principle of sufficient reason, whereas he rejects the principle of finality, of which he contests that it presents *a priori* the distinguishing marks of necessity and universality. Such a reduction limits the rôle of reason in the domain of logical operations in a fashion, whose rigour is undeniable. Even here M. Malapert shows himself to be very intransigent, inasmuch as he rejects as too loose the formula of the principle of sufficient reason: "All is intelligible" proposed by M. Fouillée after Plato and abides by the maxim of Leibnitz: "Everything that is or that is done has its reason for being or for being done thus." But, while this positive version is presented in the first book of his *Leçons de Philosophie,* which relates to psychology, one encounters a very different version in the second book in the course of the developments treating of morality. Reason, whose function and content had been so rigorously described when it was directly involved, here receives this new definition: "Reason," we are told, "is this affirmation that there must be in things a certain order that renders them intelligible."[1] And immediately there intervene these two extravagant commentaries: "Applied to the phenomena of nature, to what is independent of us, to the given, to accomplished fact, reason creates science; applied in conduct to what will be done by us if we wish it, to what ought to be or even what should be done, this same science creates morality."[2] "Do we not establish," M. Malapert will conclude, "that the moral good offers itself to us as a moral truth, which imposes itself on thought with the same character of irresistibility as objective scientific truth?" Now, is it not appropriate to recall here the rigour of the first formulas and to remember especially the maxim of Leibnitz: "Everything that is or is done has its reason for being or to be done thus," a maxim to which M. Malapert had unstintingly given his adherence, and to wonder how the principle of reason in this form would be able to accomplish the task, which is prescribed for it in the chapter on morality? How, applied to what ought to be done, will this principle discover moral conduct, if it has precisely for its object to assign its reason for being to any conduct whatever? Furthermore, how can what ought to be done be deduced from the principles of

[1] Leçons de Philosophie, p. 23.
[2] Leçons de Philosophie, p. 24.

identity and causality alone? And what a singular misuse of the word is already implied in that other enunciation that reason *creates* science! Whether it be a question of logical sciences or of the empirical sciences, what is one to do with the forms of the principle of identity or of the principle of causality, and what is here the creative element, if it is not the activity of the mind animated by the play of sensibility and the careful attention to observation? Is it not plain that the word reason is diverted from its meaning, that it no longer corresponds to anything positive. Is not the failure of every theoretical morality to be explained by the absolute inanity of the rational foundations which are supposed to serve as its supporting means?

II

M. Parodi uses analogous methods. "Without doubt," he affirms from the outset, "one can deduce nothing from pure reason, nor draw from it alone the content of morality, the code of our duties."[1] He styles such a scheme "an illusory and most absurd undertaking,"[2] and he is far too sagacious to have the presumption of a power of finality enter into a definition of reason. Let us, however, listen to him when it is a question of founding morality. Reason then becomes "a principle of discernment and of choice," which is in a certain measure acceptable, and by giving a neutral sense to these terms, for exclusion is a manner of choice, and by the mere fact of its maintaining, by the play of repetition in which it consists, the same exigencies in the heart of every psychological datum, reason automatically excludes any element not conforming to these exigencies. From there to choosing amongst the thousand elements, of which it to-

[1] Le Problème moral et la Pensée Contemporaine (Alcan), p. 110.
[2] Ibid., p. 17.

lerates the admission into the bosom of experience, there is a considerable divergence, which M. Parodi peremptorily clears by adding to the two designations we have just enunciated two new designations, one of which, at the very least, specifies the active sense that he intends to attribute to this faculty of choice assigned to reason. The sentence, indeed, reads as follows: "Reason is also a principle of discernment and of choice, a spirit of invention and of synthesis." Now, reason invents nothing, and if it is the *means* of a synthesis, but not an *intention* of synthesis, it is precisely because it never invents anything; it is because it always, in any operation of the mind, introduces some syntheses which are always the same, some exigencies which are always identical. It is by virtue of these constant rhythms of *repetition of the same* that it is for all subsequent inventions of mental activity a principle of reduction to unity, signifying what they have in common among themselves, that which, as Kant saw very well, is not lacking in any experience presented by the being to cognizance. To confound reason with the spirit of invention, is confounding it with its opposite; it is identifying the part of mental activity, that is repeated, with the part of mental activity, which is improvisation, creation of values. Now, if M. Parodi is led to make this identification of contraries, it is precisely because morality, with the valuations it implies, is contingent on that unstable part of activity, which elaborates the forms of becoming, which is creation of values and invention and because it is now a matter of arranging reason in such a way that it can enter on the same level into this new domain. In a subtle analysis, in the course of which this brusque mutation of reason in the strict sense into a reason of fantasy is accomplished, one moreover, which will be inveigled into all sports, M. Parodi endeavors to identify rational activity with an instinct. He shows, and it must be added, rightly, that rational activity is an activity and one which borrows its elements from the common seat of all activity. "An idea," he says, "once it has defined itself in us, and, having understood it, we possess it and contemplate it, can well appear like a state of repose, of inactive consciousness, of pure intellection. But this idea, whatever it may be, had to be produced, formed in us; before being contemplated, it was found and grasped; before being a state, it was an act. To think is to act and, therefore, to live." Excellent enunciations. Seen with the eyes of an idealist, for whom the movement of thought is the unique reality, they appear with all their rigor and it is from this standpoint that I applied myself, in *Les Raisons de l'Idealisme,* to showing in the movements, in the constant rhythms of thought, the circumstance which makes science possible and which permits one to comprehend in a single universe the entire ensemble of the movement subsequent upon this same activity.

One must also subscribe absolutely to those considerations of M. Parodi, according to which "analysis does not bring out any essential difference in nature or method between intellectual and sentimental life, between the inner activity, that is manifested by the idea and external life, which is manifested by movement."[1] Indeed, and from the point of view of the monism of thought, these two modes of activity are absolutely confounded. Yet they differ in a very important way on the plane of this identity. Rational activity, by the fact of its being indefinitely repeated like itself, by the fact that its very definition consists in this repetition, rational activity, although it is an act, is, by reason of the impossibility it implies of an ulterior development, as if it were a state. It is in its principle as irrational as all the rest, really a place of encounter for all the disparate elements comprised in experience, but the fact of repetition, in which its rational character consists, by which it is the form of all intelligibility, by which it is a pos-

[1] Op. cit., p. 204.

sibility of synthesis, is paramount. This fact of repetition exists and derives its originality from its banality, being a typical feature, which it is not permissible to neglect and one of an essential importance from the viewpoint of an analysis of the conditions of existence, a point of view in which all philosophy consists. Hence it is necessary, despite the identity of origin, not to confuse the psychological activity, which is repeated according to the constant rhythms of reason, from which nothing new can issue, whose entire interest and whatever it has in the way of utility consist in this crystallisation, with this same psychological activity in so far as, in each experience, it brings new elements, which can figure in these experiences or not figure in them, which can figure in them according to very diverse dispositions, which thus form the veritable content of experience, being that which differentiates every experience from any other. If one gives to one the name of reason, one must reserve for the other the name of instinct. There results from this distinction that rational activity, if it is indeed an activity, is not an instinct, but rather the contrary of an instinct.

What gives some appearance of reason to M. Parodi and renders his analysis quite plausible is that, since reason introduces into every mental operation, by the fact of repetition, in which it consists, and by its intervention in the bosom of every experience, the character of unity joining all these experiences in one universe, there is a temptation to see in it that intention of synthesis, which is precisely what M. Parodi saw in it, and thereby introduce instinct into reason. But it is making too much haste to appeal to a metaphysical providence: The fact that intuitions of space and time, that the principle of causality function in every conceivable experience is a fact pure and simple. It is the occasion of a synthesis, not an instinct of synthesis. It happens that there is in the mental play a certain number of rhythms, which one encounters in every mental operation and in which no matter what phenomenal relation is reflected. It is this encounter that makes the universe possible. It is this that effects synthesis; it is a *circumstance* and nothing more, which happens to be the means of synthesis.

Between this fact of constancy, this fact of repetition which rational rhythms are and which in the total activity simultaneously play the most humble and the most important rôle, a rôle equivalent to what is in organic life, for example, the fact of irritability pure and simple, between this quite primordial fact and an instinct, between this fact and an intentional activity, there is an interval, which is filled with quite a succession of degrees. For a moral activity to appear, in the fashion a Kant conceived it, in the way M. Parodi, M. Malapert conceive it and, with them, all rationalistic philosophers, there has to be formulated the world of sensations creating the objectivity of things, the world of the instincts from the most direct and brutal ones creating appetence for and aversion from things, to the most refined creating sympathy or antipathy of beings for beings and, at the extremity of this development, the synthetic instinct, this latest instinct to appear, the furthest from reason, the most fragile rhythm while it is the most solid ("it" is "elle," referring to reason), the most contingent and which develops in some consciousnesses and not in others, whereas it (reason) is the most immutable, the condition *sine qua non* of personality. One cannot imagine an individual who doesn't think in space, time and through the intermediary of the principles of non-contradiction and of causality. There is, on the contrary, an infinitely restricted number of men possessed of an extraordinary ardor to introduce order into that unstable part of phenomenal existence, to the formation of which the development of human activity contributes.

To confound rational activity, which is of all activities the most elementary and the most gross, with the synthetic instinct, with synthetic intention, would be the most naïve of errors, were it not the most interested or selfish one, inasmuch as moralists imagine that, by this subterfuge, they can confer the virtue of what is the most solid and the most universal to what is the most fragile, the most individual. We must, therefore, establish that M. Parodi performs the most flagrant substitution of ideas, when he concludes: "If, then, there are instincts in us contrary to reason and moral conscience, let us not fail to recognize, on the other hand, that reason itself appears as a form of instinct and thought as one of the aspects of life."[1] There results from the exposition, which has just been made, that there are no instincts opposed to reason, because instincts contrary to reason would not be a part of the universe, on which we are speculating. Hence, in order to formulate such a declaration, one must understand something quite different under the word reason from what has been comprehended in the definition of reason.

The divergence is, indeed, considerable and the contradiction absolute between this faculty to which M. Parodi, when he was considering it in itself, was denying all power of invention of ends and the thing it becomes, when it is a question of deriving morality from it: an instinct, that is to say an activity, which is precisely defined as a function with the special purpose of attaining an end. But such is always, in its last state, the procedure of faith in its effort with a view to squaring the circle, with a view to rationalizing morality, with a view to identifying the most contrary and the most extreme modes of psychological activity. It consists, we repeat, in giving or in tacitly accepting a definition of reason, in which the most rigorous critical mind would acquiesce and in making of reason, for every practical application, an entirely different use. By the first operation rationalistic philosophers put themselves right

[1] Op. cit., p. 204.

with the critical sense; by the second one they satisfy the moral sense, which, in whatever form or nuance it may be manifested, always requires the stamp of reason. By the grace of the rationalistic bias, as soon as morality is in question, the strict definition, to which they rallied, is effaced from their mind and, in lieu of this poor apparatus of control limiting itself to preventing the entrance into the mind of all notions incompatible with a minimum of reduction to unity, here we find produced, under the name of reason, a marvelous faculty, which borrows its most subtle aspects from invention, its penetration from analysis, its property of making order from faculties of discrimination and its flight from imagination. Furthermore, its power to create values by the quality of its reactions on the occasion of the objects of the external world is due to sensibility itself. Fecundated by the mysterious power, which does not cease to act in the heart of this genesis, sensibility was not long in changing into moral consciousness and conscience is still, is always, reason. From one meaning to the other of the word reason the metamorphosis is much more complete than from the worm to the buttterfly, and much stranger. And it is rather that of the "Jack in the bowl" suddenly transformed into an acrobat executing the most agile pirouettes for the joy of spectators, the most nimble capers around the little chariot with small wheels, in which just now there trailed some lucky number for a music-hall and where it could be styled the miracle of Lourdes. We shall call it here the miracle of the *Grotto of Reason.*

If such a metamorphosis is possible, if, with the faculty of illusion it presupposes, it is consecrated by so many technical theses and heavy books lending one another support, inspiring mutual confidence, it is because we are here no longer in the domain of reason, but in that of faith. A belief is a principle of hypnosis. It transfigures realities. It comes into being, itself, in the blind violence of a desire, and so it is that rationalistic faith here draws its force from the moral fanaticism created by this interest taken in the universal, in which we have already said M. Fouillée, not without reason, placed the sources of the moral instinct, this interest taken in the universal, with the particular form it assumes in every individual, who is dominated by it, and in which is expressed his most imperious will to power: will to impose on other wills, on the universe of human wills his own individual conception of becoming, and of what should be, desire to mark the development of the whole with the effigy of his individual thought. It is the passionate violence of this instinct avid to attribute to itself the prerogatives of reason, with its immutable character, with the universality of its sway, it is this passionate violence that keeps one from seeing the substitution, however crass, of one thing for another operated inside and under the appearances of one and the same word. It is this that permits one to receive as one and the same faculty the reason defined by the principles of identity and causality and the reason, that assumes the rôle of prophet through the intermediary of moral consciousness and which, under the species of the spirit of synthesis, formulates the law of what ought to be. For anyone who knows that passion plays a greater part in life than logic, that explains how, after having declared, on the one hand, that reason could never be an organ of finality, after having stipulated, on the other hand, that morality is in its essence finality, the professor of morality experiences no inconvenience in concluding that "reason remains the supreme judge in morality."

III

The case of M. Leclerc is no different. Although he finds some good arguments with which to combat the tendency of sociology to slight the individual origins of the moral fact, he is none the less one of the most positive rationalists. The title of his work, *La Morale Rationnelle,* is in itself a proclamation. In order to reinforce the tendency averred in it M. Leclerc gave as an exergue of this work the following thought of Maeterlinck: "It is in our reason, consciously or not, that our morality is formed." Now, there are in Maeterlinck, as in Tolstoy, two distinct men: one is the marvelous artist of *Pelléas,* of the *Aveugles,* of the *Intruse,* whose profound value lies in showing us well beyond reason, in instinct, in the irrational, in the *great self,* opposed by Nietzsche to the superficial *self,* the sources of reality and I regard as one of the most manifest indications of his genius the declaration he made, in the course of a public letter, that he didn't himself know the precise meaning of the symbols he uses; such an avowal implies the consciousness and the secret pride of having created something above himself. And then there is the Maeterlinck, the philosopher of the *Humbles* and of the *Temple enseveli,* in whom the divination of the poet persists, but who is not always exempt from that Christian influence turned into ideological religiosity, in which one can sense what is gregarious in the sensibility of our time. It is from the latter that M. Leclerc borrowed the exergue, which underscores the intentions of his work and this excerpt is already a manner of instituting the ambiguous game on which, as we established, every attempt to rationalize morality rests. For the term reason does not in the poet have the narrow and definite sense, which it is reputed to have in the philosopher. The poet always retains the right to metaphors, and this reason, conscious or not, invoked by M. Maeterlinck, resembles something very different from reason. This is why it admirably serves the designs of M. Leclerc, who would hesitate to give a definition of reason, which would permit one to deduce morality from it, in whom this definition is not encountered in writing, but who does not fail, when he comes to morality, to have reason intervene, as if it were understood that it possesses this creative power. At the call of morality reason indeed becomes a veritable mère Gigogne of ideas. "The good, the right and duty are ideas, which lead one another and are wielded like other ideas; one does not know reason entirely, if one neglects them, for it contains them, although it does not fuse them with the others into one whole; but they are joined with those others. By the concept of the rational, which defines the good, Morality is related to Logic and to Ontology."[1] Reason, for M. Leclerc as for M. Parodi, has certainly become a singularly enterprising instinct; it is confounded with the general activity of the mind, and the author is not afraid to divulge this conception. He expresses it with all its force in declaring: "Practical reason is theoretical reason, which continues to unfold; only it happens that in doing this it invents a concept, that has a practical application." Why does M. Leclerc not see that these two modes of activity, which he likes to identify, show their dissimilarity in the most striking fashion in that the principles of theoretical reason are universally accepted and receive identical applications at any time and in any place whereas the principles of morality are the object of the most famous dispute serving to foster philosophy and, from the diversity of applications, to which they lend themselves, give the lie most categorically to their regulatory value? Why does he not see that, if practical reason emanates from the same activity, which engenders theoretical reason, there are not in the heart of that unique activity modalities more different, more dissimilar among themselves than these two extreme manifestations of one and the same power and that, if one is called reason for its fixity, it is perhaps imprudent to call the other reason too for its instability.

[1] *La Morale Rationnelle,* p. 340.

IV

It is not only on the thought of philosophers openly lay-
ing claim to Reason for the basis of morality that rationalistic faith exercises its sway. It is, in our epoch, so prepon-
derant and it expresses to such a point a profound and
contagious state of sensibility, that one finds it also influenc-
ing speculations, whose positive character seemed best
adapted to immunize them against it. It then manifests its
intervention in places where the doctrine itself shows its
weakness, whether it reposes on a sophism until then concealed or pretends to go beyond the legitimate conclusions
it supports. Thus it is that, among recent systems by means
of which philosophers preoccupied by questions of teaching have endeavored to substitute for the theological imperative an imperative of a different nature, that of M.
Durkheim is certainly one of those that seem the furthest
removed from rationalism. For the irrational, for the arbitrariness of the divine will improvising at the right time,
in the predialectical epoch, and beyond any syllogism, the
rules of morality, M. Durkheim gives as an equivalent the
sociological imperative formulating itself also with a sovereign authority and independently of any demonstration, at
any time, in any given group. One can fail to agree with M.
Durkheim as to the modes of formation of this imperative
and see in it, instead of an irreducible and irresolvable fact,
dominating individual wills and desires from a Mount Sinai,
an abstract and dependent fact, recognizing for its origin
the conflict of individual wills, commanding these wills, because it emanates from them and, at any moment, marks
the point where they are equilibrated and stipulates the
compromise, in which they come to terms; it is nevertheless
true, whatever origin it may acknowledge, that such a fact,
exercising its authority by social pressure, commands states
of sensibility and, by virtue of these states, rules of conduct.
From the analysis of these states it is, therefore, possible

to extract a suite of precepts, on which social pressure will confer a great force and which can usefully be the object of a teaching. In that way one will, however, only teach morality already made, for it is the only one which, in virtue of recapitulation of all prior experience, can be reduced to positive formulas, the morality that makes itself explicitly dependent on another category, the category of the incalculable or of that of a creative and spontaneous activity, being at every moment or seeming to be an invention and an improvisation.

If M. Durkheim's sociological thesis presents an interest, it is on the condition of its not going beyond this limit, it is also on the condition that it does not deviate from the positive method, which he claims as his own, it is on the condition of always substituting for the consideration of psychological forces solely that of social facts. By this method M. Durkheim attains, according to me, only abstractions and I by no means think that the psychological reality, which he refuses to consider in itself, ceases to be the unique concrete reality, but, if one does not lose sight of the abstract nature of the method, if one regards as purely and simply a projection of the psychological reality the series of social facts it distinguishes and studies, this method can constitute a useful schematization, a convenient way to mark psychological reality, a precious indication with a view to determining some general modes of its development. It may be considered a grille permitting, in a certain measure, the making out of a reality, which is concealed. But one must not expect it to give more than it contains. Now, this is what M. Durkheim did, when he protested against M. Bayet's enunciations concluding, in the light of sociological theory, that the idea of duty has a purely fictitious value.

This protest against so necessary a conclusion of the doctrine is one of the most curious manifestations of the force, which the rationalistic prejudice has preserved in certain milieus. It is really quite evident that, in absorbing individual reality in social reality alone, in leaving room only for the action of the environment on the individual, without taking into account the original fact, in which the social compromise is formed, namely the action of the individual on the individual, M. Durkheim was obliging himself to consider the action of the environment on the individual as that of a physical and ineluctable law and the idea of duty as a pure phantasm arisen in individual consciousness to mask in it the play of a mechanism. In not accepting this consequence of his theory, in pretending to derive from it, instead of the science of manners, for which it serves as a most interesting prelude, a morality provided with all the prerogatives of ancient moralities, M. Durkheim condemned himself to invoking the reason of rationalists, reason in its mythological and inoperative aspect, reason under the species, in which it is no more than an impressive word and one dissembling the petitions of an instinct. To be sure, in order to conserve the former meaning of *duty,* he would, instead of establishing this pure and simple fact, namely that society, at any moment of its becoming, transmits to and imposes on the individual an aggregate of laws and commandments, have to affirm that this social imperative, with its content, is a good in itself and that the realization of this good is an end for the individual. He would also have to suppose that the individual finds in his reason a principle of justification of the social ideal as a legitimate and necessary end of his individual activity. Finally he would have to admit freedom and here we are very far removed from a positive system of philosophy. It is in this sense that M. Parodi, seeking to convict M. Durkheim of rationalism, interprets the last steps of his thought and cites from him these declarations: "Reason keeps all its liberty . . . historical genesis does not necessarily take the place of justification."

This last enunciation would indeed be decisive. The sociological thesis would, with such an avowal, singularly lose in its importance: it would resolve into a pure and simple demonstration of the value of tradition, namely of the value of the anterior empiricism: it is reason which would intervene to accord an absolute value to this empiricism, to ascribe to it the legislative character of a moral imperative. Nothing would be changed and the sociological tendency would be but one more development in the framework of practical reason.

Nevertheless, it does not seem that one would have to impute this unforeseen consequence to the doctrine. We only take it into account here in order to attest the force of rationalistic faith and to show that it still imposes itself, among philosophers, upon those who should have seemed by their previous attitude to be the most unscathed. This affirmation pertaining to the necessity of reason intervening in order to validate experience, emanates from the philosopher influenced by rationalistic tendencies, whose action it is not difficult to discern in those discussions of the Society of philosophy, in which M. Durkheim was involved and where he found himself at grips with rationalists as convinced as M. Darlu, M. Buisson and so many other educators, for whom reason in some way constitutes a working instrument with a view to that teaching of morality, which they are obliged to distribute, an indiscernible instrument with respect to which the rights of logic cease to be exercised. One could not really reproach the author of the *Règles de la Méthode Sociologique* for not always having resisted these combined or coalesced influences; did they not, for him, really constitute the most immediate form of that social pressure, of which he made a law and to undergo that pressure, wasn't it after a fashion, on his part, proving the reality of the movement, as he went along?

V

M. Belot, like M. Durkheim, intends to propose to us a quite positive conception of morality. He denies the possibility of deducing morality from pure reason *a priori* and repudiates all rationalistic ontology. On the other hand, he contests the sociological viewpoint of M. Lévy-Bruhl and reproaches the science of manners for "making moral rules appear irrational at the very moment when it explains them." This consequence, however, ought to be considered by M. Belot an attestation in favor of the excellence of the method, if he was truly persuaded that morality is not to be deduced from reason. This objection on his part would, then, signify a contradiction in his thought if, like all the philosophers, who have just been at issue, he didn't also take the word reason in two different senses. There is for him pure reason, and there is also that reason which is the ensemble of the faculties of the mind striving to adapt a means to an end and which intervenes in all operations, whatever they may be, of mentality. It is at the cost of this ambiguity that he presumes to reconcile reality with rationality. In so far as he rules out the intervention of reason (pure reason), M. Belot affirms that ends are not demonstrable, are not objects of science, and he holds morality to be, in its essence, finality. Thus he digs the abyss, which he is going to ask rationalistic sophistry to help him clear. Hindered by the antagonisms, which he has just shown as chains at his wrists, how will he succeed in modeling that positive morality, for which he is searching? How will he discover the end, which will give a meaning to morality? How, situating that end in sociality, will he differentiate his point of view from that of the sociologists, which he has condemned? Persisting at first on the road of a rigorous logic, M. Belot is of the opinion that the end required by morality to constitute itself is given in man's will, in the will, that then is to say in desire, for what is a will, which isn't stretched on the spring of a desire? Hence one would immediately have to recognize that here is the beginning of the domain of the diverse, of the unstable and that the moral end is at every moment determined by the more or less sharp conflict entered into by the diverse tendencies, in which human will and desire are expressed. It was when arriving at this same dialectical stage that free, to be sure, of any concern for teaching, I distinguished, with the phenomenon of manners, in order to oppose it to the category of logical deduction, a new category, that of conflict. M. Belot stopped short on this slope.

Resuming the habitual procedure of rationalists he set out in quest of a principle of unification in a domain whose nature it normally is to produce the modes of diversity, and there follows the series of sophisms he had to bring into play in order to accomplish this task. It seemed to him that the constitutive end of morality, engendered at its source by the human will, was given, in a general form, in social experience. Now this is true, if it is a question of the concrete, unstable, diverse end formulated *at any moment* as a resultant by the conflict of individual wills. But, by social experience, M. Belot means to designate the social fact itself *in abstracto,* social life, and social life detached from becoming, where it is transformed at every moment—immobilized, in the abstract—presently appears to him to be the common condition of all activities and of all human ends whatever they may be . . . "As soon as one wants something, one desires in principle society."[1] And society appears to M. Belot, in so far as it is a means for all ends, whatever they may be, as an end common to all wills. Now there we have a really exorbitant misuse of words: from the fact of a means being common to dissimilar activities, it does not become an end for these ac-

[1] Quoted by M. Parodi in *Le Problème Moral et la Pensée Contemporaine,* p. 93.

tivities. Horses engaged in one and the same race all use their legs to accomplish the distance of the course and arrive at the goal. However, it will not be enough in order to win the race, which is the true objective of the test, for them all to make use of their legs; each will have to strive to make a better use of them than the others and if there is a winner, if the end is attained by one amongst them, it will be because it proved itself to be the best runner. Such a conclusion is the more unexpected in M. Belot, since he recognizes the necessity of defining morality by its matter, by its content and not by its form. Now, wishing society, whatever may be the thing that one wishes, from the mere fact that such a will is implicit in every particular will, to wish society, according to that signification of the term, could never be anything but the form of morality, a form in the cadres of which morality, in its essential reality, would appear as a competition between the different conceptions of the society, in which the diverse tendencies are expressed. The fact of wishing society would not even present any interest in a human wishing, since no will could elude this necessity; but the peculiar fashion in which the individual would like to realize society would be the only thing to consider, that is to say the element of conflict and of diversity that this willing would introduce into the general phenomenon, in which the relations of concrete individuals constitute the purely abstract entity that society is. The notion of society, then, could in no way provide us with a practical equivalent of the good in itself of metaphysical moralities, since the abstract entity, in which society consists, can adapt itself to the most diverse realizations in the same way as a Louis XIV table is a table, as well as an Empire table or a kitchen-table, whereas the Good in itself would be, if it existed, something definite demanding identical modalities for all activities.

Until now, however, and if he thinks that, with the social fact taken in itself and *in abstracto,* he has assigned an end for morality, M. Belot has not introduced reason into the affair. Wherein, then, is his system, which up to this point is purely sociological, going to give access to reason? By entrusting to reason the care of adapting society, seen as the universal means, with perfection to the diversity of human ends. Now, as society will be indifferently the means of any end whatever, which trial alone will decide, which conflict alone will settle amongst the different ends formulated in intention and desire, reason is here a word to designate experience, or else it is a faculty to create ends independently and without the concurrence of trial and conflict. Here, then, it has become with this power to engender means, that which had in the first place been affirmed that it was not.

When the different ends of action will have been discovered, whether by experience or by the mystical intervention of reason, it is still reason, according to M. Belot's theory, which will take care of discovering the best methods. Diverted from its only legitimate meaning, reason has come here to signify no more than a technique. And that is the last state of the rationalistic belief in its attempts to justify itself theoretically. Such endeavors always result either in attributing to reason, in its relations with morality, a power which it had been denied, when it was a question, on the threshold of the theory, of a pure and simple analysis of reason, or in the employment of reason in the sense of that complex activity, which man calls into play in whatever enterprise he may be engaged. In reality the theorists of the rationalistic belief almost always use these two subterfuges at one and the same time: while they stun the mind with the noise of their protestations against any ontological or teleological use of reason, they do not forget to secretly make use of it to their profit in order to give a content to their thesis, and at the same time, in order to divert the attention from this maneuver, they hasten to employ the word reason in the most commonplace sense. It is in this last sense that M. Parodi, apropos of M. Belot's doctrines, invokes in favor of morality a quality of rationality, when, after having termed an illusory undertaking and even absurd among all others the one, which would consist in wishing to deduce morality from pure reason, he adds: "But one cannot construct or organize anything without it (reason) either." It is only too true and that is the way it is, whether it be a question of tracing the itinerary of a journey, of driving an automobile or of having a soft-boiled egg cooked. A rational morality, in this sense of the word, has exactly the value of a corset or of a pair of suspenders equally rational, just as prospectuses drawn up in honor of certain commercial brands affirm with an equally good right.

Is there any need to specify again the meaning and the importance of this study on the *rationalistic faith*? Must it be formulated that this critique of rationalism is the reverse of a critique of reason? Is it also necessary to declare that, in taking away from morality the support of reason, one does not intend an act of hostility against morality? This affirmation is, without doubt, more necessary than the other. The effort of professional moralists with a view to deducing morality from reason has come to the point of being so persuasive that the fate of morality could appear to be tied to the possibility of this deduction. Now, to morality one has to apply Nietzsche's fine observation relative to the meaning of existence: "One interpretation alone was ruined, but as it passed for the only interpretation, it could seem that existence had no meaning and that all was in vain."[1] The relation of dependency between reason and morality formed in the mind by the teaching of moralists is the most illusory notion imaginable, for there are no categories more distinct

[1] *La Volonté de Puissance,* t. I, p. 46.

one from the other than that of reason and that of morals. In regarding the value and the legitimacy of morality as inhering in its connection with reason moralists have, therefore, shown themselves to be the worst enemies of morality, inasmuch as they were making its existence depend on a condition, which sooner or later had to prove inexistent. But the failure of this pretension does not entail the failure of morality. Morality is a fact, which is not at the mercy of a theory or of a false attribution of origin, a fact of sensibility requiring no recourse to reason to affirm itself. It is acting as a moralist in the true sense of the term to destroy a legend and to withdraw morality from the realm of the universal and the absolute, in which it is not susceptible of any application, in order to situate it in the domain of contingency and relation, where it does at least rediscover the activities, which really beget it as the condition of their play in its form judged to be the most perfect and which they intend to perpetuate.

Part II

SPIRITUALISM AGAINST THE SPIRIT

CHAPTER I

A COUNTERFEIT OF THE DOCTRINES OF REASON AND OF THE MIND

I.—The postulates of the official philosophy.
II.—The doctrine of freedom.
III.—The realism of the *adaequatic rei et intellectus.*

"We no longer have an official doctrine and no one, I imagine, regrets it."[1] Thus M. Parodi expresses himself at the beginning of his latest book. In this double assertion there is a part of truth and this can at first delude. The philosophical doctrine, which had for several centuries been reigning in the University, has, it is true, lost something of its tyrannical character. It does leave room for the expression of viewpoints very divergent from its former canon, and to this the work of M. Parodi bears witness, whose author, by his official function, is qualified to be an interpreter of University thought. M. Parodi has indeed, in his interesting inventory, exposed contemporary systems of philosophy and set forth in all their relief, according to conscientious analyses, theories whose logical development implies an evident contradiction with the old official conception. Thus, more particularly, M. Durkheim's sociological theses, to which he attributes the important place due them and whose consequences he scrupulously deduced in what they have that is contrary to the traditional spirit.

[1] D. Parodi, *La Philosophie Contemporaine en France. Essai de Classification des Doctrines.*

Nevertheless, it seems that one must not take literally this first part of M. Parodi's assertion: "We no longer have an official philosophy," and this impression results not only from the conclusions of the work formulated in terms of spiritualistic rationalism, but also from the angle from which the different systems are appraised and held to be favorable or contrary to the presumed aim of philosophy.

So, having formulated that we do not have an official doctrine any more, M. Parodi adds: "No one, I imagine, regrets it." And, here again, I would not be able to support this estimation, if M. Parodi did not hasten to attenuate it and to complain, with more than one good mind, he says, that we do not have "a definite and imperious philosophical tradition, which disciplines and sustains intelligences"[1] either.

Taking up again on my own the two terms of this assertion and modifying them according to my personal viewpoint I shall say that there is good ground to be pleased that the former scholastic conception in philosophical matters is really close to waning and that one could wish it to be definitively ruined. On the other hand, it would be of the most extreme importance for this declining doctrine to be replaced with another. The defect of an official conception certainly does not consist in its being a force and a commanding one, but in the fact that it commands in an incoherent fashion and gives inexecutable orders. Considering the works of a very great interest, that have seen the light under the régime despite the constraint of so baleful a directing principle, one is justified in forming the highest conception of what philosophy could be in France, if the individual efforts dedicated to its service were to find a principle of coordination in the official organism, whose intervention can sanction, accredit and favor their expansion; it would be desirable for them to receive from

[1] Ibid., p. 7.

the latter also a program tracing the cadres of the task to be accomplished with a view to the aim envisaged and clarifying the nature of the philosophical task itself with a clear definition.

Since this study has for its object to criticize the general directions of the official philosophy, no work could furnish me with more authoritative indications than that of M. Parodi, nor be of a more precious avail by its qualities of clarity and composition. By its general conclusions, by the angle from which he considers and evaluates the philosophical systems of the last thirty years, he does, indeed, permit one to discern what still is, at the present time, the philosophical doctrine of the University. But he offers, besides, for the general study of contemporaneous philosophy, a great convenience from the fact of the classification he establishes of these systems according to their natural affinities. As a matter of fact this classification remains valid in the greater number of cases, even when one considers the philosophical manifestations of our time according to other principles of appreciation, so that this new view encounters, amid the outlines instituted by the author, groupings all made of systems, to which it applies broadly according to the new incidence it determines.

In rendering this homage to M. Parodi I mean to address it to the methods of the University themselves, as regards the ensemble of tools and the formal qualities, with which they endow minds and with respect to the intellectual enthusiasm they realize, but it is not without opposing to these fortunate results the weakness, or better, the defect of coherence of the general doctrine in the service of which they are applied. What does, indeed, strike one in reading this philosophical inventory, is the high individual value of a great number of French philosophers, their power of invention and their creative force in comparison with that poverty of the leading idea destined to orient their efforts. And this is even accentuated when one puts face to face,

in M. Parodi's work itself, the fine order of the classifications, the art and the clarity he evinces in the course of the
exposition of the systems and the ambiguous character
of his conclusions, in which a personal ingenuity nevertheless shines forth, whose valor is compromised only by
the obscurity of the doctrine and its manifest ineffectual-
ness. There are unequal struggles and the illogical, which
doubtless has its place in life, is, in the intellectual order,
too heavy a weight for the better mind to be able to bear
its burden.

I

What is, at the present time, still the official doctrine of
the University, is spiritualism. But this spiritualism is a
counterfeit of what this doctrine would be, if it were understood according to the etymological signification of the
term designating it. Etymologically spiritualism promulgates
the doctrine of the spirit. Under a more adequate designation it would be what idealism is in the philosophical sense
of the term, in which Berkeley employed it, *a doctrine
according to which there is in the world only thought* and
which from the first presents an immense advantage: for,
by the monism, which it institutes, it allows one to confront
on one plane and embrace in one and the same universe,
an ensemble of phenomena which, by reason of their common nature, do not exclude *a priori* the possibility of a
coordination, of a general explanation and of a philosophical systematization in terms of one another. Now, in
school or academic language, according to the acceptation
in which it has been taken since the Middle Ages until our
day, and in which usage, stronger than logic, compels its
employment if one wishes to be understood, it has been
transformed into precisely the contrary of this coherent
conception, having come to designate *the doctrine accord-*

ing to which there exist in the metaphysical universe two principles, matter and spirit, between which there is no common measure and which are separated, like an impassable abyss, by a difference of an absolute nature. The question being posed in these terms, it pertains to philosophy to demonstrate how one of these principles acts on the other, how the spirit introduces order into the material world and makes morality reign in the given universe. Under these conditions, what can philosophy be? No more than a sport, an intellectual exercise perhaps very fitted to sharpen and supple the mind, but a mode of activity powerless by definition and, by virtue of the rules of the game, incapable of ever attaining its object. One could compare it to a foil in fencing where the two adversaries, despite all their skill and all their ardour, will never be able to pierce each other's hearts and, by all their feints, their blows and clashes of steel, their free movements and their direct hits, will never arouse in the spectator, all emotion being ruled out, more than an admiration of initiated connoisseurs.

In searching into the question how so useless a game and one of such evident inconsequence can hold in history the rank one finds it occupying, one is led to discover a new characteristic feature and one of the most important of official philosophy. Under the appearances of a science inspired by a concern for knowledge it is, in reality, a mode of activity inspired by the social instinct in so far as it sets itself up as a directing principle, provided with the knowledge of good and evil, as an authoritative principle having the mission of governing men for their greatest good. Philosophy has from its origins, and by virtue of its explicitly utilitarian and social character, put the moral problem in the first place of its solicitudes, and this problem is decided by a decree of the social instinct, whose imperious and arbitrary quality M. Durkheim acknowleges. If philosophy afterwards appeals to reason, it is because it has recognized in reason an intellectual principle, which, in a certain realm, exerts an imperative action of great force on men's minds. Instead of inquiring into the question of the limits, within which this action is legitimate, which will be the belated work of critical philosophy, it has had no other concern than to extend those limits to the objects relating to its own domain in order to make the latter benefit by the imperative power, of which reason disposes. The product of this police-operation is rationalism, which is, with respect to reason, what spiritualism is in reference to the spirit, an usurpation of a name for the purpose of an exploitation of influence and of prestige.

The quite arbitrary manner in which the moral problem, in its political form, was from the outset substituted for the problem of knowledge, explains how this problem could have been posed in terms as paradoxical, as irreducible the one to the other as those of matter and spirit. It was of little consequence that the solution of such a problem was logically impossible, since an arbitrary decision of the social instinct was to settle the question in sovereign fashion. And it was even preferable, in view of such an eventuality, for the intervention of reason to have been precluded from the start.

This it indubitably was from the beginning, and had it continued to be that way, there would have been no official philosophy; there would have been an official dogma, first theological and eventually sociological, promulgating imperatives without taking the trouble to justify them. If it was otherwise, that no doubt happened through a sort of laziness of the dogmatic will, yielding to the law of the least effort, seeing in reason set up and designed to that effect an aid which, acting in each individual mind, would exempt it from an effective intervention. Thus with those thrifty municipalities which, in order to save the employment of some agents, entrust the lawns and grass-plots of the city's gardens to the protection and superintendence of the public itself. It is to this method that we owe the whole abstract mythology represented by official philosophy, which has, at the same time, compelled philosophy, as a science of knowledge, to assume a critical appearance, a negative character, which are not its true nature, but come to it from the necessity of dissipating the phantoms engendered by spiritualistic metaphysics.

If one has long imputed to philosophy being the servant of theology, *ancilla theologiae,* if this imputation, when one goes to the bottom of things, has not lost its truth, one can say with equal exactitude that theology was itself the servant of the social instinct and of political power and that it constituted itself with a view to a moral action and not to answer the need of a metaphysical concern, which true religion is in its essence. Dominated by this social preocupation, it could have founded itself on character revealed, that in which its doctrine took pride, in order to impose its viewpoints. Now, it is curious to observe, and this remark attests the extraordinary prestige exercised by reason on men's minds, that it was theology that first appealed to the arguments of reason to bolster dogma. Philosophy will only follow it on this path, on which this counterfeit of reason will be realized, which official rationalism, adapted to the service of the spiritualistic myth, has become. Indeed, throughout the Middle Ages and up to the Seventeenth Century, one sees two conceptions opposing each other and vying for supremacy. And the one represented by Duns Scotus, William of Ockam and Roscelin, tends to place above the laws of reason a divine arbitrariness, which alone gives these laws their value, while it maintains them, and which can also overturn them. And the other, which is based on the authority of Saint Thomas Aquinas and answering Scotism with Thomism, immobilizes the divine will in rational laws, places reason above divine arbitrariness. It is this double adverse tendency that one would again easily find on the one hand

91

in the thought of Pascal and, on the other, in the heavy dialectics of Bossuet. Now, between these two tendencies, of which one situated dogma where it was safe from the enterprises of the critical spirit, it is the other which, letting human reason penetrate into the sanctuary of faith, introduced into it its most dangerous adversay, which the Church hallowed with its approbation. It seemed more profitable to it to recognize the rights of reason than to openly alienate a power, which had so much influence over minds. It judged it to be easier to disguise it and to enthrall it to its designs than to combat it openly in its integrity. Whence that rationalistic spiritualism, which it bequeathed to the University and which the latter only succeeded in changing into a spiritualistic rationalism by an inversion resulting only from the shifting of the tonic accent and the role of sentinel attributed to reason in the theoretical conception, in order to conciliate the growing number of minds won over by its ascendancy.

II

In the doctrine of the University, as in that of the Church, the moral problem continues to hold the first place, and it is the salient feature of these two teachings that liberty, in the sense of free will, is in them really more or less secretly, but with an equal force of attraction, the aim toward which all the efforts of dialectics tend. Two substances being given, matter and spirit, between which there is no common measure nor, by definition, any possible relation, liberty is the act, by which the mind has the ability to command matter. Such is, in the crude light of the absurd, the character of the spiritualistic undertaking determined by dualism, which is its point of departure and by the secret intention, which exploits the doctrine to the advantage of a social interest: for, with liberty, with the responsibility which accompanies it, one installs fear of chastisement and remorse in the heart of every man, like as many supports of morality, like as many invisible agents, and which do not trim the budget.

This quality of absurdity, apparent in the light of the principle of contradiction, few philosophers of the school have had the courage to contemplate in its logical nudity and, if Bergson dared to say: "every definition of liberty will corroborate determinism,"[1] it is because he thought he had found a means of proving liberty without defining it, which amounts to a new way to burke the question. The classical means of disguising this problem and of screening its shocking absurdity consists, for the philosophers of the school, in persuading themselves that freedom commences where necessity ceases, that liberty is exactly the contrary of necessity, as if there were opposites, as if, from the logical negation of the existence of something there had to arise the positive notion of some other thing, as if reality let itself get caught in the artifice of these snares, as though it sufficed to demonstrate that a thing is not produced in such a way to know how it is produced, in order to render comprehensible by the mind what until then was incomprehensible by the mind, as if it was enough to demonstrate that Pierre is not in Paris to know, at the same stroke, where he is and on what street he lives, of what city of the vast world.

It is, nevertheless, on the naïveté of such an hypothesis that the entire official dialectic is based, that fencing-foil dialectic. which always substitutes for the reality of the aim to be attained the plastron of some fictitious object, here for the demonstration of liberty, the demonstration that the chain of causal necessity presents some solutions of continuity, is broken in some places. M. Boutroux, with

---

[1] Quoted by M. Parodi, p. 270.

his thesis on *The Contingency of the Laws of Nature*[1] furnished the model of demonstrations of the sort. With that clarity of method, which one would like to see in the service of better causes, he pointed out the different hiatuses where the causal chain conceals from the mind the link, by which it connects one series of phenomena to the antecedent one. There would, strictly speaking, be no reason to object to such a demonstration if, after having beaten in this series of open doors, M. Boutroux did not pride himself on discovering, amid the intellectual darkness brought about by these analyses, liberty in the sense of free will, in a phantom, in which we recognize only too distinctly our ignorance of the way things happen. With a frankness, for which one hesitates to either praise or criticise him, M. Boutroux administers to contingency the baptism of liberty, of which the demonstration is the secret thought and the raison d'être of official philosophy, *ancilla imperii,* the handmaiden of political power.

This frankness is not habitual with the representatives of the University philosophy, and the same reason making me hesitant to praise or criticize M. Boutroux for the one he manifests inspires in me the same hesitancy to qualify this habitual dissimulation. For it is a question of not putting reason and the critical mind to too tough a test. If it remains a thing understood among initiates that liberty will take the form of free will, when it is a question of using the notion with a view to the needs of morality, that ulterior design remains hidden in the course of the analyses, in which this more sober and more positive school-exercise is accomplished: to search into the weaknesses of causal explanation, with a view to introducing into the metaphysical universe a principle independent of necessity. Thereby the scientific appearance of these dissertations is saved. But here it is important to publicly expose the sub-

[1] Alcan.

94

terfuge, to which those lend themselves, scholars and future masters, who have the family spirit in order to caution those who, not being preoccupied only with being good pupils, have a true taste for philosophy. Now, whether it be a question, with M. Boutroux, of contingency or, with M. Renouvier, of new beginnings, what one must hasten to point out before the accomplishment of the substitution of a mythological object for the object attained by demonstration, is that such hypotheses, granting that they correspond to real metaphysical events, have nothing in common with liberty in the sense where this indefinable term implies free will and responsibility. Whether it be a question of the universe, of the metaphysical being or relates to the psychological ego, the fact of there developing in them a decision or a principle of action independent of any motive or any antecedent does not imply any appearance of freedom or responsibility in the subject in which or in whom this event arises. For the event arises or does not arise—whether the subject wishes it or not—and upsets—whatever he may say or do—without the consent of his will and his desires, his will and his very desires. Outside of any possible or even conceivable intervention, the event assigns to him a new role, which he did not choose and which it isn't up to him to discuss.

The introduction of liberty into philosophy, therefore, constitutes the most exemplary of sophisms. Now, this step also reveals, one couldn't forget it, the most characteristic feature of official philosophy and in which stands out the moral solicitude, of which it is the result.

The problem of knowledge only comes in second place in these preoccupations. It appears too late, when the perspectives among which it is going to be posed, have already been altered by the dualism inherent in the doctrine. The absolute and irreducible heterogeneity of matter and spirit really does not fail to diffuse on this already intricate question a definitive obscurity, which the lightning of faith alone can streak with some brusque clarity. It is the gleam of this lightning that theology has transmitted to modern philosophy. Having the hypothesis of divine beneficence enter into the concept of divine perfection, theologians did not want to believe that the creator of human intelligence fashioned this intelligence with a view to duping it with mirages. They made a dogma of *the adaequatio rei et intellectus,* of the exact correspondence of objects to the representation, which is formed of them in the mind and throughout the *Somme* (Summa Theologica of Saint Thomas, the vision in God of Malebranche, and the preestablished harmony of Leibnitz, there filtered first a realism of the material object and then of the general idea, of which the official philosophy received and conserved the deposit. It is this tradition, with which minds are entirely impregnated, that will permit it, on the one hand, to elude the problem of knowledge with respect to material objects and, by introducing into pure reason human conceptions of order and of morality, which are utterly foreign to it and are formed in the realm of human sensibility, to transpose on the plane of historical realities a messianism of reason, according to which, in despite of the protestations of experience, the world would develop spontaneously toward ends of order and harmony.

False spiritualism masking the dualism of matter and spirit, despotism of moral solicitude setting up the demonstration of freedom as an essential aim of the doctrine, false rationalism attributing a moral content to reason, such are the features to which I have just called attention in the official philosophy and the ensemble of which really has the physiognomy of a doctrine. They all proceed from one and the same fact, namely that, in the struggle between the Vital Instinct and the Instinct of Knowledge, whose vicissitudes, as shown in my work *From Kant to*

Nietzsche, compose all the phases and all the episodes of the history of philosophical ideas, official philosophy always was and still is at the present time the protagonist of the Vital Instinct. And, by vital instinct one must understand that pragmatic instinct, which is embodied in all forms of social, religious or political volition, which sees in its impulsions the norm of existence and immediately makes intelligence itself subservient to the presumption of utility, which its own activity generates. Far from using it as a marvelous apparatus of vision, permitting one, which is all that philosophy consists of, to distinguish the real amid perspectives which must be respected, thus to know in the measure in which it is possible, how things happen, the vital instinct mutilates the mind, fashioning it in such a way that it makes the law of things appear such as it has conceived it itself and as it wishes it to be. Accepting this thralldom official philosophy ceases to be philosophy.

Chapter Two

THE CHARACTERISTIC FEATURES OF THE OFFICIAL DOCTRINE IN M. PARODI

I.—From the author's personal enunciations.
II.—From his estimations of philosophical systems.

I

That the official philosophy corresponds to the description, which has just been given of it, is what the declarations contained in the work of M. Parodi, confirm, as well as the estimations of different groups of philosophical systems, which appreciations reveal the point of view inspiring them. These enunciations do not admit of any ambiguity. Thus, as M. Parodi formulates in his conclusions, "in rationality determination and liberty, intelligibility and novelty seem to meet."[1] "Being and thought," he will also say, "are no doubt but one and the same essential reality, nature is a profound and universal aspiration to consciousness, a need for order, an existence wishing to become thought and therefore already is potentially, a spirit that is searching itself, a liberty which, in order to grasp and possess itself, fixes itself in concepts and binds itself by laws."[2] And don't we have there, functioning in the heart of existence, this rational automatism ready to in-

[1] Ibid., p. 483.
[2] Ibid., p. 492.

99

troduce into the play of the Universe the moral ideas which in the last lines of the conclusion, appear as the justification and the aim of philosophy. "To recognize and to show more and more," the author proclaims, "that if all this vast universe is the work of spiritual liberty, it must be penetrable to the mind; it is thus that we view the proper work of philosophy and its destiny in the future, as it has always been in the past. . . . It is not by chance that the same word idealism expresses the doctrine, according to which reason everywhere finds itself at home in the very heart of things and at the same time the practical effort toward an ideal of justice and of "beauty."[3] And in such citations, which it would be easy but useless to multiply, are encountered all the features noted in the course of the preceding analyses as characteristic of the spiritualism of the school. And in them one also finds, developed to perfection, that ability to conceal or ignore what is too gross in the posing of the problem; thus with this dualism of spirit and matter, of which one no longer dares signalize the irreconcilable antagonism, which is discreetly hidden under that spiritual freedom making of the universe its work, against which no condemnation is pronounced throughout the entire work and which, being the very principle of the doctrine, is carefully dissimulated, as if it were also its shameful and compromising part. One also finds in it, applied with an extreme finesse, that other procedure characteristic of the method and of the official tactics and which consists in annexing to the false spiritualism given to minds as pabulum a whole philosophical vocabulary, implicitly stripped of the profound meaning, by which it won over minds, but utilized for the sway it exercises on these intelligencies. The Roman Caesars acted in a like manner, when they opened the temples of the city to the alien gods for the authority they exerted on the con-

[3] Ibid., p. 295.

quered peoples, by which they became intermediaries of the power and of the means of government. And thus with that idealism invoked in the citations, which I just borrowed from the work of M. Parodi, whose logical virtue and explanatory power would seem better applied if put in the service of a doctrine accepting none of the premises on which the idealism is founded and to which it owes its rigor. The same could be said of that idealism celebrated in such able terms that a superficial or even an inattentive mind runs the risk of accepting the assimilation concluded in a turn of phrase and which requires that one recall to one's mind the express postulate of spiritualism, that dualism of body and spirit, which is essential to it and which idealism formally rejects—in order to dissipate the mirage created by the exploitation of common notions or notions affirmed to be such. Through such artifices the sense of words is, imperceptibly, changed and one has idealism say, as one had rationalism say, something quite different from what is contained in a doctrine of the spirit or in a doctrine of reason. At the same time, by means of these insignia, and thanks to the dusk, one has gotten into the school minds, who are surprised and some of whom do not notice the different arrangement of the separate divisions and that they are in a temple dedicated to morality, instead of being in a bright study room.

But it is not only idealism that M. Parodi strives to annex to this spiritualistic rationalism of the official doctrine. It is, besides, any other point of view suited to ennobling by its prestige and fortifying by its authority and its credit this doctrine of the school. It is, among others, intellectualism, which is a name for a philosophy of pure reason, a name around which some minds had gathered after the school had pillaged this term of rationalism in order to place in it in the natural shell of a doctrine of reason a doctrine different in all respects. And, as for idealism, this annexation is employed by means of simple

101

juxtapositions of terms taken as homonymous in the course of a correctly phrased sentence. "Ours is a period of anti-rationalism, or at the very least of anti-intellectualism"[1] M. Parodi will say, attributing to the two notions, intellectualism on the one hand, and rationalism in the University sense on the other hand, one and the same meaning, thus inflicting on the first term the treatment, which was already inflicted on the second, and a little further on accentuating the same confusion: "Pure rationalism subsists," he will enounce, "and perhaps the reaction against anti-intellectualism is at hand."[2] Finally, still with the same intention and according to the same procedure: "Only," he remarks, "from 1870-1890, French thought was still clearly remaining fundamentally intellectualistic and rationalistic,"[3] as if intellectualism, in the positive sense it has kept for many minds, were not diametrically the opposite of rationalism such as the school prepared it beyond all the positive forms of reason.

II

If the distinguishing marks attributed to spiritualistic rationalism were not found again in M. Parodi's explicit declarations, they would still appear with an irrecusable evidence in the tenor of the classifications relating to the different philosophical systems exposed and grouped in his work. These classifications, with the evaluations accompanying them, are indeed strictly determined by the dogma of adequate knowledge and by the doctrine of liberty. In order to understand and interpret them one must, besides, never lose sight of the alteration in meaning, going to the

[1] Ibid., p. 17 or 18.
[2] Ibid., p. 70.
[3] Ibid., p. 90.

point of inversion, inflicted by the School on such doctrines as rationalism and intellectualism. This alteration accepted by M. Parodi, who employs these terms in their modified signification, could alone explain to me how, devoting to my own viewpoints a few lines of his analyses, he was able to class among anti-intellectualistic systems a philosophy, which lays claim to the most intransigent intellectualism. As to this, in default of the theory of Bovarysm itself, irreconcilable with Bergson's hypothesis of intuition, the terms, explicit as any ever were, of my introduction to my first work, would attest.

But, in the view of M. Parodi, in that of the rationalism of the University, the possibility of a knowledge adequate to its object including the adaptation to an end of the activity of existence is an essential postulate of intellectualism. Consequently the classification in the group of anti-intellectualistic systems of the philosophy of Bovarysm is explained, inasmuch as its maxim: *Everything that knows itself knows itself other than it is,* categorically excludes this possibility. When I oppose to official philosophy the principle of another philosophy I shall search into the question, if it is not this partial agnosticism, which is alone consistent with a doctrine of pure intellect. At present it is sufficient to note that, dominated by that conception of knowledge adequate to its object as the philosophical aim to attain, M. Parodi classifies among the anti-intellectualistic systems, in so far as they defeat that postulate, an entire group of doctrines and investigations, of which it must be established that they bring a brilliant experimental confirmation to the axiom of Bovarysm.

M. Parodi rightly reserved a very careful examination for epistemology, that science which, in the extension of the *Critique of Pure Reason,* institutes the critique of the value of science and, by the importance of the scholars and philosophers applying their meditation to it, holds a first class place in the cycle of speculative thought of these last thirty years. Thus he has grouped all the works of this order under the common head of a critique of scientific mechanism. Now, under this designation, which has the merit of posing the problem in its most urgent aspect, it is indeed a question of a critique of the value of science and of the value of knowledge, if one admits that scientific knowledge is only the development of common sense and that there is no mode of knowledge outside of this common knowledge. Now, what M. Parodi establishes in the course of this examination of contemporary criticism, is that, the more serious and scientific it becomes, the more it demonstrates the deficiency of mechanism as a principle of explanation of the universality of phenomena, the more it makes apparent its incompetence to embrace existence in a system of laws, where existence is revealed to knowledge according to its identity or is reflected as in a mirror according to its exact resemblance.

M. Boutroux' thesis on contingency distinguishes all the solutions of continuity, which are manifested between the divers orders of phenomena and seems to prohibit science from analytically deducing the ones from the others. Anticipating the theories of Bergson, M. Hannequin notes, amid the cadres traced by M. Boutroux, the impossibility of making the continuity of sensation accord with the discontinuity of the atom. Now, "to fail on the continuous, is to fail on reality," M. Bergson will subsequently emphasize. So that, instead of that *adaequatio rei et intellectus* postulated by the school, here is affirmed, paralleling the progress of the critical mind, the *inadequatio rei et intellectus*. Throughout the course of M. Meyerson's fertile analyses in his fine work on the theory of science,[1] M. Parodi encounters the same conclusions. For these analyses, taking everything into account, promulgate the irreducibility of nature to

---

[1] Meyerson, *Identité et Réalité*. See also by the same author: *De l'Explication dans les Sciences*. 2 volumes.

science. Mathematician and philosopher, M. Gaston Milhaud declares that there is logical certitude only in the order of concepts and constructions of the mind, certitude vanishing as soon as the laws of the mind are applied to an empirical content. Finally M. Henri Poincaré, whose renown as a great scholar but lately gave a considerable reverberation to his conclusions, M. Henri Poincaré brings out a disagreement between the simplicity of scientific laws and the elements, to which they apply—things—which indubitably "are not simple." And it is this divergence between things and the representation of things in the mind that M. Parodi sees extending more and more through the analyses of Duhem, of Borel, of M. Ed. Le Roy, those scholars, who decree the symbolic, approximate or purely conventional character of science.

Now, what is the attitude of official philosophy before these avowals of pure scientists joining philosophers, expressing approval in a chorus with them and in a still more resounding voice, to confess the inability of science, the most objective knowledge there is, to grasp reality according to its identity? This attitude is ambiguous, for the positions of official rationalism are such as not to permit them either to rally to these points of view or to condemn them categorically. As a matter of fact the critique of the savants substitutes for the dogma of adequate knowledge the presumption of inadequate knowledge, and in their theses this presumption assumes all the appearance of a demonstrated truth on the firmest data of mathematical experience. So, as a man of too perspicacious a mind to contest the value of these demonstrations M. Parodi confines himself to seeing in them a menace to intellectualism, using this term in the sophistic sense of the school, and he expresses the wish that a new progress of analysis may succeed in filling up the intervals revealed by criticism, in its present state, between reality and the law, between the object and the notion. Having shown himself to be faithful to the doctrine and to the terminology of the school by attributing an anti-intellectualistic character to epistemological criticism, M. Parodi is nevertheless careful not to excommunicate the adversary. Without yielding anything on the doctrine, he spares the latter the support of the force, which combats it today. In expressing the hypothesis that, from the development of criticism itself, there can result points of view, disclosing to us paths of communication between phenomenal series separated by impassable gaps in terms of present knowledge, he reserves the possibility of a future alliance. Moreover, he adopts a very prudent attitude. For, if it betrays and points out the stroke, it insinuates at the same time that the contest isn't over. Now it is the advantage, and this must be the supreme maneuver of the one who feels the game to be jeopardized, to gain time or to act in such a way that it never terminates. In chess it is to seek a stalemate in order to avoid a checkmate.

By means of this respite, amidst the indefinite expectation wagered on this messianism of an intellectual order, official philosophy knots an imbroglio, creates an equivoke, from which one of its most essential dogmas benefits. If, indeed, epistemology, if the critique of men like Poincaré, Milhaud, Meyerson checks the dogma of the adequate, it does with the hiatuses, which it makes appear in the chain of necessity, open intervals, kinds of vague terrains; in these, by the procedure, whose sophism I have already analyzed, the philosophy of the Vital Instinct will cultivate liberty, as if the contrary of necessity were necessarily liberty; and from this liberty, in at first an indeterminate sense, will issue free will and all the condiments of morality, which has remained under the ensign of philosophy, the true commodity, which it is a question of introducing into people's minds.

Thus one can explain M. Parodi's almost neutral tone with respect to this epistemological criticism, whose recent steps he sets forth in the best light. If the critique of scientific mechanism imperils the dogma of adequate knowledge, it opens a door—the philosophers of the University do not wish to see that it is a blind door—to a theory of liberty, to morality, to the imperialism of the Vital Instinct. It is through this blind door that the philosophy of Bergsonian intuition will slip in. Where savants and philosophers, where a Poincaré, where M. Milhaud, Duhem or Meyerson stick to establishing the inability of knowledge to embrace reality according to its absolute identity and do a work of strict intellectualism, Bergson introduces a new faculty, intuition, an old term taken in a new sense and until then not in common use, by which the mind would realize this adequate knowledge, inaccessible, as M. Bergson demonstrates with perfect sagacity, to ordinary intelligence. In order to render it assimilable to intuition the philosopher of the *Données immédiates de la conscience* fashioned a new mode of reality, a reality from which he eliminated quantity, spatial time and the discontinuous, in order to allow to subsist in it only quality, duration and continuity. Escaping the powers of intelligence, taking flight between the meshes of the concept, this reality, on its author's assertion, can be grasped in its absolute identity by intuition penetrating it and confounding itself with it. Inasmuch as these theses are known, I shall not dally discussing them here, as it is my intention to criticize them, when I oppose to the postulates of official philosophy and the rationalism of the University the sober philosophy of the intellect. Here I do not wish to retain more than this fact: the complaisance of the official philosophy with reference to the theses of M. Bergson, although they are in as formal a contradiction as possible, in avowed and proclaimed contradiction with the intellectualism, on which it prides itself elsewhere. M. Parodi, however, recognizes

107

that it is in this philosophy that "anti-intellectualism reaches its culmination."[1] And he discerns very well the inanity, all things considered, of Bergsonian intuition. In any case he does, indeed, formulate that, if intuition, in M. Bergson, is not pure incognizance or absence of judgment, to which it sometimes seems to tend, if we think we can grasp it like that nebulosity surrounding the pure kernel of intelligence, "it is by the truth that it can only be grasped in contrast, in opposition to intelligence and, therefore, in its rapport with the latter and thanks to the latter."[2] But this lucidity, which does not go to its logical consequences, fails to bring about the radical condemnation, which Bergson's philosophy should incur from the representatives of a University having for its mission to distribute a philosophical teaching and the definition of its object. By situating the object of philosophy outside of the knowledge by concepts, M. Bergson really situates it outside of any possibility of its being taught. "A new philosophy, which would place itself, according to its very definition, in the extra-intellectual matter of knowledge by a superior effort of intuition with a view to the possession of the mind by itself"[3] would have no more than the name of a philosophy. It would belong to a psychological gymnastics, whose supreme exercise, this torsion of consciousness on itself recommended by this master of a new mysticism, would only, were it possible to suppose it realizable, lead to a perilous leap outside of the limits of knowledge, into the world of ecstasy or the annihilation of nirvana.

If official philosophy did not absolutely repudiate these practices, which would substitute for the teaching of philosophy a kind of fakirism and transform the school into a

[1] Op. cit., p. 344.
[2] Ibid., p. 343.
[3] Ibid., p. 256.

108

mystical sect, it is for the same reason, but much stronger here, that kept it from pronouncing the anathema against the critique of philosophers and scholars, breaching the dogma of adequate knowledge. If, indeed—though strictly negative and uniquely concerned with defining the true character and the limits of knowledge—scientific criticism, interpreted by the desire of spiritualistic philosophers, had suggested the thought to them that it would be possible to introduce freedom by the gaps established in the fabric of causality, M. Bergson brought a much more positive support to the thesis of liberty; expressly; he destined a place for it in the play of a reality conceived according to its veritable essence and cured by his ministrations of the folly of number and the delirium of space. If, furthermore, M. Bergson, in terms as explicit as those of a Poincaré or a Duhem, judged in substantial analyses—and which remain the valid part of his work—in favor of the necessary inadequacy of knowledge realized in intellectual terms, was he not, on the other hand, promising to attain the absolute of knowledge by a new way and did not this community of the object aimed at deserve one's showing some indulgence as to the means of the enterprise.

Of the foregoing observations there should be retained that the philosophical inventory drafted by M. Parodi reveals to us two facts of great importance: on the one hand, the high development of the philosophical mind, which, for thirty years, has been manifested in a flowering of systems of a rare fecundity—and one could not express too much gratitude to M. Parodi for having brought this wealth under the public eye by grouping, arranging and exposing in his work the elements composing it;—on the other hand, the inability of the official doctrine to give a general meaning to this effort, to assemble in one symphony the multiple accents of contemporary philosophers, in short to make these individual endeavors, in which there scintillate so much strength and such beautiful gifts, converge toward one and the same aim.

Therefore M. Parodi, in this abundance and this multiplicity, through the perspectives of the official dogma, discerns especially diversity and variance. "Our teaching is none the less divided," he says, "among several opposed tendencies . . . it would be puerile to deny that our students of the Sorbonne or of the Faculties of the provinces are by that very fact solicited in contrary directions."

He sees in these symptoms a crisis of philosophical thought and, if he immediately defines this crisis as a crisis of growth, it is because optimism is an official virtue and not because he perceives the principle of synthesis, which would tomorrow be able to unite this multiplicity of tendencies into a living organism. If so lucid a mind finds it absolutely impossible to discern that genesis, it is for a reason more grave than the want of an official doctrine. It is, conversely, because there still exists an official doctrine and, as was indicated at the beginning of these pages, with the hypothesis of a dualism of matter and spirit, with the usurpation and the deformation of viewpoints such as spiritualism, rationalism and intellectualism, it propounded the philosophical problem in insolvable terms and confused the perspectives, through which it can appear in its true light and become comprehensible to the mind, in the measure in which it can be effectively grasped.

A PHILOSOPHY OF PURE KNOWLEDGE

In terms of the postulates of the official philosophy, it is then impossible to form a synthesis of the works, of which M. Parodi allows us to glimpse the wealth. Must one, then, renounce any design of gathering the fruit of this speculative activity, which not only for thirty years, but for almost a century, outside of the school and in opposition to its directions, has assembled the materials of a coherent philosophical science, whose different parts constitute an aggregate susceptible of being the object of a positive teaching? To pose the question is to determine the reply. It remains to seek out the guiding idea which, without being publicly formulated and without being authoritatively promulgated as a rallying-signal coordinating the efforts of all, has inspired each individual effort, as if it were the necessary consequence of the entire past of knowledge. And this idea is the one which, doubtless on account

111

of this general determinism. inspired in me this conception of *Bovarysm,* which indeed seemed, when it came to my mind, like a creation and the expression of my sensibility, but which subsequently became for me a directing principle, whose living logic dominated this individual sensibility, that had engendered it and imposed on me, sometimes rigorously, on some points, in the name of reason, conclusions different from those which my natural tendencies would have dictated to me. In the name of reason and in terms of the strictest intellectualism, but these terms being taken in the pure sense, which they implied before having been adapted to its needs, to the point of inversion, by the official philosophy.

This conception of *Bovarysm* has sometimes been understood in a restricted sense, by reason of its literary connections and because I produced it first in its psychological aspect and in the manner of moralists, according to the acceptation in which La Rochefoucauld and Vauvenargues are moralists. Its import, however, is entirely metaphysical and I give it here such as it appears in the different works, in which I exposed and developed it,[1] and as if the term by which I determined it drew its entire signification from its definition alone, as if the word *Bovarysm* were a word made out of whole cloth exempt from any prior designation to express something else. Now, if Bovarysm, psychologically speaking, is *the fact according to which man conceives himself other than he is,* Bovarysm in the metaphysical sense is *the fact according to which existence necessarily conceives itself other than it is.*

Applied to the phenomenal diversity in which existence is manifested, the formula is transformed into the following one: *Everything that knows itself knows itself other*

---

[1] See *Le Bovarysme, la Fiction Universelle, les Raisons de l'Idéalisme,* and in *La Dépendance de la Morale, le Commentaire aux Raisons de l'Idéalisme.*

than it is. In this triple aspect Bovarysm is founded on Idealism considered as monism of thought such as it was conceived by Berkeley and whose axiom is set forth as follows: there is no existence without the knowledge that this existence has of itself, so that existence, given in knowledge, is a fact of thought. It is the objective aspect of thought. Knowledge is its subjective aspect. The world is thus given in the indeterminate relation of thought with itself. It is in this sense that I situated its genesis in a movement of division of thought with itself. But thought drawing from itself the two terms, in which it represents and realizes itself, necessarily conceives itself according to the formula of *Bovarysm,* other than it is, in an approximation. For the part of itself, in which it makes itself subjective in a state of knowledge necessarily escapes the knowledge it takes of itself, necessarily and indefinitely, whatever be the number of the relations, which thought may fashion with itself.

Such a point of view and one based on strict psychological empiricism, which idealism is, may be said to be opposed in two ways to the doctrine of the University. Excluding, with the monism of thought, the difference of an absolute nature between matter and spirit, it renders logically possible this construction of existence, in which the philosophical endeavor consists. On the other hand, for the presumption of an adequate knowledge it substitutes, drawn from a logical deduction, the principle of a knowledge necessarily inadequate to its object. From the standpoint of a philosophy which, inspired by the instinct of knowledge alone, has no other concern than to distinguish how things happen, the *adaequatio rei et intellectus,* which to official philosophy appeared as the aim proposed for philosophical effort and as the solution the problem of knowledge, shows itself to be a confusion of the object and the subject of knowledge, in which all knowledge is abolished and, by the application of the idealistic axiom, all existence also.

113

Here then, in the light of this new mode of evaluation, we have a complete inversion of the valuations relative to the philosophical facts noted and classed by M. Parodi in his inventory. Thus it is, more particularly, that all the criticism of the value of science, such as it was directed with such conscientiousness and brilliancy by men like Poincaré and Duhem and the most undaunted scholars of our time, and whose conclusions constituted a defeat for official rationalism, is in accord with the principles of a philosophy of pure reason. An unfavorable symptom in the light of the first point of view, it attests, in the light of the second viewpoint, that the human mind has in our day, in some of its best representatives, attained a period of maturity and that, freed from the presumption of knowing beyond the limits of possible knowledge, it has become wise enough to discern reality in its mobile and positive features. Thus, as an attentive observer, it is able to recognize it in the fleeting approximation, which the play of thought gives him thereof, while the latter creates and fashions it in the endless movement, in which it divides itself into object and subject, escaping continually by the agility of that flight from the nothingness of identity.

In terms of this philosophy of knowledge, the critique of the value of science, accomplished by the savants and the philosophers, whose endeavors M. Parodi grouped in the chapter entitled *Critique du Mécanisme Scientifique,* assumes, instead of a negative character, an explicitly positive character. When M. Poincaré infers a divergence between the simplicity of the law and the complexity of things, when M. Milhaud signalizes the disappearance of all certainty as soon as one applies the laws of the mind to an empirical content, when M. Meyerson declares nature to be irreducible to science, and when in the view of MM. Duhem, Borel, Ed. Leroy, science assumes a symbolic, approximate or conventional character, all these verifications, all these ways of seeing agree with the perfectly logical deduction, which the philosophy of Bovarysm formulates in this maxim: *Existence, conditioned by knowledge of self, necessarily conceives itself other than it is. Everything that knows itself knows itself other than it is,* such maxims expressing at the same time: that a state of knowledge is realized, and that it is realized in an approximation. If the theory draws from the logical principles, on which it is based, an *a priori* value, independent of experience, it must be established that the critical epistemological conclusions present a perfectly orthodox character and are what one could wish them to be. If one takes the theory for an hypothesis drawing its value and its degree of certitude—that is perhaps the most modern fashion of envisaging the question—only from the extent of its capacity for explanation, one has to confirm that these conclusions of the critique strongly attest in its favor. M. Parodi, although he did not, in the several pages devoted to my viewpoints, mention this conception of Bovarysm under which all those other points of view are ranged, nevertheless amplified further the importance of these conclusions by recapitulating the most general tendency of the contemporary mind in these terms: "An infinitely various and mobile reality," he noted, "and a thought which, in order to recognize itself in it, to dominate it and to use it, tries to impose upon it the simplicity and the homogeneity of its conceptions or of its laws, but thereby travesties it and denatures it, such would be the latest conception, toward which our epoch tends."[1]

The observation is true. Yet it is important to distinguish what meaning philosophers attribute to the terms *travestir* and *dénaturer*. Is it a question of a pejorative sense, according to which the knowledge gained by this

[1] Ibid., p. 474.

intervention of the concept would be disqualified? This is the case with certain philosophers. This is, indubitably, the case with M. Bergson. Is it, contrariwise, a question of a simple verification relative to the nature of knowledge and its objective description? It is in the second sense that the formula of Bovarysm should be understood. A positive sense and one, which does not in any way incriminate the mechanism of intelligence.

Existence, conditioned by the knowledge of self, necessarily knows itself other than it is in the unending movement of division of the object and the subject. Thereby it realizes its perennity, assuring itself against any possible end. At the same time it creates for the spectator, for the scholar, for the artist an innumerable sequence of states, all given in the unstable relation of the object to the subject, unamenable to the effort, which would abstract the pure object from the relation, in which it is engaged with the subject, and embrace it in the absolute of the law. Hence knowledge is always inadequate to its object, but, thus constituted, it is all that it can be and this approximation, grasped by common sense or by science, exhausts the entire matter of knowledge.

All the criticism of official philosophy that I instituted in the first part of this work, *Rationalism Against Reason,* and which I have pursued in the course of these pages, belongs under the invocation of this thought of Pascal: "The final step of reason is to know that there is an infinity of things, that surpass it. It is quite weak, if it does not go that far. One must know how to doubt where it is necessary, to make certain where it is called for, to submit where one should. Whoever does not act in this manner fails to understand the force of reason." By instinctively submitting to this discipline I was led to recognize in this limited and approximate knowledge, deduced from

116

the principles of reason, the whole of knowledge. Now it happens that the principle of this limited knowledge allows one to coordinate the philosophical effort accomplished in nearly a century and to discern, under some divergences, which other perspectives made appear irreducible, its fundamental unity.

Thus the critique of scientific mechanism of men like Poincaré, Milhaud and Meyerson proceeds entirely from the positive viewpoint, which has just been opposed to the critique with a pejorative tendency of M. Bergson. There is really no reason whatever to suspect these savants of having undertaken this task with the aim of depreciating knowledge and, on the contrary, everything attests that they placed themselves opposite science itself just as they are accustomed to face and contemplate particular objects of the sciences with the aim of defining them exactly, of determining their properties.

Beyond this critique of the last thirty years the theoretical principle of inadequate knowledge sanctions the most important result of intellectual evolution in the course of the Nineteenth Century, the *acquisition of the sense* of *the relative* such as it developed in a Taine or in a Renan, such as it would be easy to distinguish it in its literary and psychological manifestations in the novels of Stendhal or in the criticism of Sainte Beuve, such finally as it has been propagated in the public mind to the point where the notion of the universal relativity of all things figures in the class of the commonplaces of our time. Commonplace, indeed, a universally accepted notion, which scarcely anyone contradicts, but which for all that did not bring about the considerable transformation which it implies. This is owing to its failure to be sanctioned in the speculative domain by an official initiative and because a guiding thought, qualified by the powers at its disposal to exert a strong influence, was not able to draw from the state of fact realized by a spontaneous development and from that maturity acquired

117

by the greater number of minds the results, of which these phenomena admit. Accepted, recognized, even extolled in the philosophical milieus of universities, too astute to be inscribed against its evidence, the notion of relativity has nevertheless been ignored in so far as it would have been a question of determining by its light the great directions of teaching and of philosophical research. In metaphysics and in morality one has continued to speculate as if things were given us in the absolute, as if we had to find in reason, the all powerful intermediary between this absolute and its phenomenal manifestations, the laws of action and of an adequate knowledge.

Hence the principle of knowledge necessarily inadequate to its object brings to the movement of thought clearly conceived for a hundred years the theoretical ratification, which the contrary dogma still in force in official thought was refusing it.

But to sanction with a theoretical view the analyses of epistemology judging the value of the scientific laws to be only approximate, to embrace amid its perspectives this notion of the relativity of phenomena and knowledge, which for an entire century has filtered through the thought of philosophers so as to penetrate little by little into the majority of cultivated minds of our time, is a significant step. Clearly it is but a progression toward a conception, which in the history of philosophy of these last hundred years has had a considerable reverberation, though unequal to its importance, and whose fortune is still to be made: it is the conception of positivism, which we owe to Auguste Comte.

Positivism is the establishment and recognition of experience as the unique source of all knowledge. The diversity of things cannot be deduced. This is what the theory demonstrates and what criticism establishes. Consequently experience accumulated in observation remains our only way of access to the knowledge of phenomena.

By it we attain the relations they constitute and according to the fashion, in which these relations are repeated, with more or less constancy, more or less like themselves, they furnish knowledge with more or less fixed guide marks, on which it is erected in its entirety with its varying degrees of probability and of approximation.

The positive mind, such as it was conceived by Auguste Comte, conforms exactly to the maxim of Pascal. He may be said to have accomplished the final step of reason, inasmuch as he knows that an infinity of things transcend it and henceforth no longer asks it to decide in realms, in which an initiative rules, that escapes him.

It is to the development of the positive mind as much as to M. Boutroux' doctrine of contingency, partly confirmed by scientific criticism, that one must attribute that specificity of the sciences, which M. Parodi notes as a progress in the course of his inventory. And that specificity was practised in a domain of great importance, which official philosophy had hitherto annexed to itself in order to introduce into it that usage of reason condemned by Pascal because it implies ignorance of the limits of reason. This domain is that of morality, which MM. Durkheim and Lévy Brühl treated as a science pertinent to given facts in the most complete empiricism. One finds, I already noted, in the work of M. Parodi an excellent account of the doctrine of M. Durkheim. But, if the critic was able to attribute to this doctrine the importance, which it really gained by its breadth and its documentary wealth, the spiritualistic philosopher—I also noted it, but it is important to insist on it—felt ill at ease and was unable to draw from it the logical consequences, of which it admitted and which assume a great interest. This is why he emphasized with complacency the effort, by which M. Durkheim, induced by his University connections, set himself in spite of the gods to make up a rationalistic physiognomy for his thesis. Shall I say, as for mysef, that the sociological theses of M. Durkheim are of the sort, whose tendencies of a strongly individualistic sensibility dissuaded me, but of which, under the influence of the philosophy of Bovarysm, I had to acknowledge the legitimacy. Now, from the standpoint of inadequate knowledge, the criterion of this philosophy of Bovarysm, it is not by attenuating the particularity of the different points of view of philosophers and of scholars that it will be possible to realize their synthesis, but that reconcilement will be obtained in the light of a guiding idea worthy of accomplishing this task only by exalting the originality of each one and pushing their logic to its radical consequences. With respect to the moral phenomenon, the function of reason, according to its legitimate employment, is expressly limited to recognizing that the genesis of this phenomenon goes beyond the use of reason, that it is produced according to the play of an experience, which is determined in the social environment by the contribution and the conflict of individual sensibilities favored or disserved by the climacteric transformations, intellectual or technical, which can affect this milieu. Hence reason teaches us that morality cannot be deduced from reason and that is its final step. In order to be informed on the moral phenomenon it only remains to cull in experience the modalities which it has assumed in it. Far from reason determining these modes, it is experience alone, in so far as it repeats itself and, by repeating itself, hardens itself, that introduces into morality rules, which, by their fixity, come close to rational rhythms. By this observation of the facts one obtains the matter of that science of morals, to which M. Lévy Bruhl, who by his works on Comte and positivism was predestined for this task, devoted one of his most important works.[1] But this science does not exhaust the nature of the moral phenomenon. If, by taking into account the degree of constancy of the observed facts,

[1] Lévy Bruhl, *La Moral et la Science des Moeurs*, Alcan.

it permits one to base on the calculation of probabilities certain inductions, of which some are strong enough to legitimatize a teaching, it nevertheless leaves room for an element, which does not appertain to the hold of any science, because it is not yet given in experience, because it belongs to the reality that is in the making and is the very gesture of becoming. It was for the purpose of reserving its place for this modality of existence that, in *La Dépendance de la Morale et l'Indépendence des Moeurs*, I ranged morality, considered in its genesis, under the category of conflict. It is during this conflict between sensibilities that certain forms of morality relevant to particular modes of action, whose norm was not stratified in the course of the preceding periods, are sketched out, elaborated and established. It is with an analogous intention that M. Albert Bayet in *L'Idée du Bien* refers to a morality of infraction, which is doubtless the most active manifestation of moral ferment and in the name of which refractory sensibilities, at times at the cost of considerable risk, again call into question rules of conduct, which did not receive from anterior conflicts a sufficient sanction and one to guarantee their reign.

Without doubt it is, for a philosophy of state, annoying for things to present themselves in this unfinished aspect, that they should move and transform themselves and not lend themselves to the application of definitive rules of administration. Thence the tendency of this philosophy to extend the jurisdiction of reason beyond the limits, in which it commands; thence these moralities termed rational, in which the rules of morality are seen to be deduced from a principle which, under the banner of reason, dissimulates a fact of authority inspired with more or less success by the imperialism of the vital instinct. There, to be sure, it is a question of an imperialism analogous to the one animating any individual instinct avid to dominate and to impose its own valuations, but of an imperialism which, to borrow Carlyle's vocabulary, is here produced in its vulpine form. A philosophy of knowledge animated by the sole concern to know how things happen has no motive to thus corrupt reason, to misuse its prestige and its name for undertakings of domination foreign to its object. It is, to the contrary, ready to accept, outside of the circle where reason can inform it, what experience gives in the way of information, and, when experience in its turn fails, it has no inclination to ask more of it than it can give, but it still satisfies the instinct leading it to know that life here has the word in the form of action and desire and that experience cannot be anticipated. This is why the valuations of such a philosophy of the systems of morality will differ from those of the official philosophy. Far from attenuating the empiricism of M. Durkheim's sociological morality, it will approve it only when pushed to its extreme consequences. And, likewise, it will not class among the anti-intellectualistic theses or as contrary to reason those of M. Blondel, M. Le Roy or M. Georges Sorel to the extent that they discover the sources of action in a region, in which the fruits of intelligence are not yet ripening. One could not invoke too frequently or with too much insistence the maxim of Pascal, which is the shortened formula of the purest intellectualism and the purest doctrine of reason. Intellectualism, as the application of the principles of reason, does not consist in explaining everything by reason, but in singling out domains, in which reason commands those subject to another principle. It is by this insight that one avoids compromising reason in adventures, in which the misuse made of it can only depreciate it, and that one stands a chance of discovering a principle of explanation applicable in these realms. The mere consideration of the disorder and the incoherence reigning in the sphere of moral phenomena would suffice to inflict a definitive discredit on reason, if one had to believe with rationalists that reason holds sway in it.

III

Philosophers such as MM. Le Roy, Blondel, Duhem, Georges Sorel, Jean Weber, and one can add to their names that of M. Poincaré, whose declarations with respect to this are formal, recognize in short, that the causes of action derive from a source situated well above the place where reason is formed. Hence they show themselves to be intellectualist philosophers. They are, in the true sense of the term, rationalists in the measure, in which they attribute an irrational origin to morality. Of their doctrine a philosophy of knowledge could only criticize certain tendentious features, which they would ascribe to this causality of the act, strictly speaking unknown in its essence, and the pretension they could express of drawing from these features the elements of a new modality of knowledge. This restriction poses the question of philosophies of intuition and particularly that of Bergsonian intuition, to which M. Parodi has devoted a large place in his exposition of systems. Now the portion of the incalculable, which the philosophy of knowledge deduces as essential to the fact of existence given in becoming, were it even from the analysis of the principle of causality,[1] really implies the unascertainable character of action. But, if by this very fact it admits the insufficiency of determinism as a principle of explanation of the totality of the phenomenal flux, it rejects for the reasons previously formulated the explanation by liberty, as soon as this term, void by itself of any meaning and which is unable to receive one from any definition, nevertheless pretends to acquire a positive sense by the imaginary consequences imputed to it with the idea of responsibility and the moral sanctions implicit in this idea. This settles the question of the relations of existence,

[1] See *La Loi de Constance et l'Inalculable* in *Comment Naissent les Dogmes*.

in the metaphysical sense of the term, with that part of itself, which is the individual act, and determines exactly in what measure the philosophy of knowledge admits or rejects the conclusions of the philosophies of intuition in so far as they apply themselves to explaining the genesis of action.

As to what concerns the modes of knowledge, it is the cornerstone of the philosophy of knowledge that there is no other knowledge possible than that inadequate and approximate one, which is formed in the indefinite series of relations of the object to the subject. This principle does not tolerate any compromise with the hypothesis of Bergsonian intuition. Some philosophers, M. Julien Benda among others and principally, have criticized the philosophy of M. Bergson in the detail of its constructions. It would be very difficult for me to believe that these criticisms were not largely justified, since from the viewpoint of pure reason such as I developed it in opposition to the philosophy of practical reason, which is the official rationalism, Bergsonian intuition, supposing that it attained its object, would be realized in the confusion of the object and the subject, in the suppression of the relation of one to the other, outside of any possible state of knowledge.

Besides, there are two parts to consider in M. Bergson's philosophy. One is, in the language of the metaphysician and the logician, of the same significance as the critique of thinkers like Poincaré, Milhaud, Duhem and Meyerson. In it M. Bergson was anxious to demonstrate the inadequate nature of scientific knowledge. *L'Evolution Créatrice,* which was my first contact with the thought of M. Bergson, contains some remarkable analyses on the cinematographic character of scientific mechanism, on the impossibility of expressing the continuous in terms of the discontinuous. These analyses, entirely conclusive and of a great force, had struck me as perfect illustrations of the Bovarysm of knowledge, only whereas, in the light of Bovarysm, the rough estimate attained in scientific approximation constitutes all the knowledge realizable by the mind, whereas the two notions of the continuous and of the discontinuous are in it like the two branches of a gripper, between which reality, which is neither continuous nor discontinuous, can be grasped, for M. Bergson the continuous is reality itself. It is in criticizing this conception, according to which a means of constructing reality is taken for reality itself, that I called the doctrine of M. Bergson a realism of the continuous.[1]

It is there indeed a question of an operation of the mind analogous to the one by which the realists in the scholastic sense of the Middle Ages, attributed a positive reality to abstract ideas, to general ideas, in which nominalists rightly saw but a means of constructing intellectual reality and handling it. It was in order to grasp this phantom reality reduced to pure duration, to quality and to the continuous, conceived outside of space and of quantity, that M. Bergson invented Bergsonian intuition. One must, of course, designate it by the name of its creator, the term having till now received diverse significations, of which some are quite acceptable, but which M. Bergson for his part would not accept, because they imply a state of knowledge subject, as for its definitive realization, to all the conditions of common knowledge, that is to say intellectual knowledge, and with the relative and only approximate character peculiar to it.

Now the aim of M. Bergson is to embrace in intuition a state of absolute knowledge. In the fashion of official philosophy he means to realize the *adaequatio rei et intellectus*. His entire effort is one seeking to elude the relative character of all knowledge and bent on eliminating from the act of knowledge one of the two terms, in which the relation is formed. When, like a magician intent on the philosopher's

[1] *Le Réalisme du Continu (Revue Philosophique* au 1er Janvier 1910).

stone, he endeavors to exorcize from the immediate data of consciousness space and the concepts to which it gives rise, quantity, number and the discontinuous, his aim in the last instance is to base knowledge outside of the relation of the object to the subject, to situate it in a state of absolute confusion between the one and the other. Bergsonian intuition, then, is the leap into the absolute. For the subject of knowledge with a view to intuition it is a question of bounding and transporting himself integrally into the object. But M. Bergson does not, in the course of his analyses, ever accomplish this perilous leap to the end before his public. He does not loop the loop. He evokes the exodus of the subject toward the object up to the limit where something still remains of the subject outside of the object, little as it may be; but this subjective intervention still suffices for the determination of the fact of knowledge in the relation of the object to the subject, that is to say in the intellectual sense, the only one accessible to the mind, whereas the extreme amplification of the objective portion gives the impression of a more adequate knowledge and suggests to dazzled eyes the illusion that everything would go far better still and that the adequation or equivalent would be perfect, if the subject were entirely resorbed in the object. That is the second part of the philosophy of M. Bergson, and, whereas in the first part he applies himself to fixing the limits of reason, to showing the inadequate and necessarily inadequate character of knowledge, he reveals in this second part that he does not accept this fatality of the relation, according to which existence, in order to possess itself in knowledge, represents itself in its own view in an indefinite series of states of knowledge, not one of which exhausts its reality, which all attain to resemblance, without ever being able to equal identity.

Whereas philosophy consists in enquiring how things happen, M. Bergson adopts an entirely different attitude: he revolts against reality; he wishes things to be different than they are, and one can say of his system that it is the last great effort of the theological mind with a view to attaining the absolute through the perspectives of a reality, of which the essence is relation, phenomenal character. When M. Bergson sets himself to abstracting from given reality one of the terms of the relation, in which knowledge is formed, he is suppressing the conditions of all knowledge. Far from attaining existence in its identity, he is casting existence itself into nothingness, if, according to the idealistic axiom, existence is conditioned by knowledge of self, and the absurdity of such a consequence is enough to demonstrate the artificial nature of the undertaking.

Therefore the philosophy of knowledge would not be able, with respect to the Bergsonian philosophy of intuition, to manifest the same indulgence, which official philosophy has evinced. This indulgence is explained in that, with the doctrine of liberty or that of adequate knowledge, in spite of the difference of the means employed, M. Bergson's theses bring a support to the postulates of the official philosophy, which the original novelty of the dialectic and the seduction exerted on many minds by the philosopher's ability seem to render precious. More preoccupied with imposing its points of view than with knowing in the speculative and disinterested sense of the term, a philosophy of state was not able to find in the principles inspiring it the reasons, which would have decided it to reject this support. The philosophy of knowledge, governed by an entirely different conception of its rôle, can not do otherwise than reject completely the second part of the philosophy of M. Bergson. It must do it with all the more force because, by the vogue, which the talent and the gifts of its author have brought him, as well as the mystical tendencies, for which it appears to give new pretexts, this philosophy is a menace to the sense of relativity, whose development is the great event of the mental history of the last century.

Hence the valuation of philosophical systems in the light

of the philosophy of knowledge determines this final difference from the valuations, which the criterion of official philosophy inspires in M. Parodi. Whereas the philosophy of knowledge attributes a positive value and an efficacious action, with a view to the constitution of knowledge, to the epistemological criticism of the last thirty years, to the theses considered by M. Parodi to be the most subversive, those of MM. Le Roy, Blondel, Georges Sorel or Jean Weber, while save for some restrictions it welcomes as very important contributions to a strictly empirical conception of existence the Mobilism of M. Chide or the Pluralism of M. Boëx-Borel, it is compelled to denounce the philosophy of Bergsonian intuition as the most contrary to the aim of philosophy and, under the semblances of the newest procedures, as the most dangerous for the advent of the new philosophical spirit.

IV

To recapitulate the different features, which constitute for the philosophy of knowledge its own physiognomy and to evoke the diverse orders of phenomena which it coordinates, I shall formulate these few propositions:

1. The philosophy of knowledge brings to philosophy that specificity, which the official philosophy lacked and which is the mark of a science that has reached its maturity. As a matter of fact it restricts philosophy to the determination of the power and of the limits of our faculty of knowing.

2. Based on psychological experience, it is a pure idealism. It does not infer from the datum in knowledge a thing having an existence independent of the act of knowledge in which it appears. Thus it is a monism of thought, so that existence conditioned by knowledge of itself is manifested in it as the very movement by which thought, drawing from itself the two terms of knowledge, object and subject,

128

spectacle and spectator, invents, models and makes appear the cinematographic imagery of the real in the indefinite of relation, in such a manner that no end can be assigned to this metaphysical game and that knowledge realized on the plane of these indefinite relations can never be adequate to the object of the universe. Each image appearing in the succession of these particular relations itself participates in the inadequate nature of this metaphysical knowledge by itself, but this succession of states of inadequate knowledge itself makes up the whole texture of reality, and this series of approximate clichés, in which it develops, gives knowledge such as it is, in the approximation in which it consists. Hence the criticism by scholars of the value of science, far from bringing out the impotence of science, indicates its perfection. By discovering, in the course of its analyses, that science attains phenomena and their laws only in an approximation, it reveals that knowledge thus realized is all that it can be and all that it should be.

3. As for what relates to reason, reducing to a minimum the resort to the *a priori,* the philosophy of knowledge seeks its origins in the play of experience itself and identifies it with the most constant rhythms engendered by the movement of thought. Commenting on this theory of reason set forth in the Introduction to *Les Raisons de l'Idealisme* and in the ninth chapter of the same work, I noted in the first part of this work "there must be and it is sufficient, for knowledge such as it is given us to be possible, that there exist in the mind invariable rhythms always repeating themselves similar to themselves, in terms of which other unstable and perpetually changing rhythms are assembled in a suite of representations having a common bond. . . . We do not go out of given experience to attain the one kind or the other kind, which differ among themselves only by the constancy shown by some and the whimsical multiplicity, which characterizes the others."

129

4. When one does not make of reason a theological entity through which human voices make themselves heard issuing decrees dictated by the political and religious instinct inflated by a presumption of social utility, there is no reason whatever to imagine that these invariable rhythms which we style reason determine, as to their form and their individuality, the more or less unstable rhythms, which develop above them and for which they purely and simply serve as a prop.

The rhythms of time and space, in which Kant saw the forms of pure reason, do not in any way condition the properties and the qualities of the bodies, which are formulated in extension and in duration. In the principle of each category of phenomena an arbitrariness intervenes, and the fact that phenomena develop amid these perspectives, if it has as a consequence integrating them all in one and the same universe, does not in any way imply that a bond of causality exists between them and these elementary and constant rhythms. It results therefrom, these constant rhythms assuming the rôle of pure reason on the theme of an absolute idealistic empiricism, that one cannot deduce from pure reason any of the categories of phenomena, which the rationalism of pure reason, founded on an arbitrary extension of reason, makes the gesture of deducing from it. Therefore the developments of idealistic empiricism result, through the perspectives of the doctrine of the inadequate, in the ratification of the positivism conceived by Auguste Comte.[1]

At its point of juncture with positivism the philosophy of knowledge determines the attitude of the mind with

[1] M. Louis Weber in another way, reached the same conclusions clearly intimated in the very title of his work: *Vers le Positivisme Absolu par l'Idéalisme.*

respect to different categories of phenomena, of which it points out the distinguishing marks in the play of experience. Corresponding to the specificity of the philosophical object, it traces more particularly the limits of cognition in its relation with action and with desire in its extreme form, in which it generates belief and faith. Positivism, and this is wherein it coincides with idealistic empiricism, is really a philosophy of experience subject to the strict rule formulated by Pascal, provided that one replace in his maxim the word reason with the word experience. Experience, indeed, must not be interpreted, any more than reason itself, beyond its own data. Thus, when it makes us attain those constant rhythms of thought, to which idealistic empiricism gives the name of reason, Pascal's maxim at the same time forbids our attributing to those rhythms a more extensive influence than they have and to liken other less essential rhythms to them. Of whatever order of phenomena, that may be under consideration, it enjoins us to adjust the degree of probability of the knowledge we can acquire of these phenomena and of their laws to the degree of constancy, which, as experience apprises us, these phenomena exhibit as to their modes of production. The maxim here regulates the attitude of the doctrine with respect to knowledge.

Inasmuch as existence is produced in our sight in the movement of becoming, the maxim also prescribes that we distinguish, among the categories of phenomena, those whose rhythms are crystallized in the "devenu" (what has become) from those, which, belonging to the "what has become" by several of its manifestations, are also formulated, on the confines of becoming, in an aleatory game, which confers upon existence one of the most characteristic features of its physiognomy. And here the maxim affects the attitude of the doctrine with respect to action and also the sciences treating of action, those which claim to determine its rules and to influence its orientation, par-

131

ticularly morality and all the sciences that have received the name of moral sciences. It reminds us here that experience cannot be anticipated, that there is no science but of what has become and that in certain domains it is not a question of knowing in order to act, but of acting by virtue of a preference, the causality of which plunges into the incalculable and which, having been manifested in the act, will be able eventually to enter as a document into the body of data of science.

Finally Pascal's maxim determines the attitude of the doctrine in regard to the religious fact in the metaphysical sense of the term and such as can move all individual consciences, leaving out of account the positive religions, whose rôle requires another valuation with regard to the positive spirit.

From the fact that existence conditioned by the knowledge of self is compelled by the conditions of knowledge to conceive itself in the indefinite of relation there results that there is not, among the roads and paths of knowledge, any way of access toward the absolute, in which the religious fact in its metaphysical aspect consists. Therefore one can establish of any conception, in which the human mind would pretend to situate the religious fact, that it is either constructed in violation of the rules of knowledge and escapes all intelligibility, or that it presents to the credulity of men an object, which has nothing comparable to the metaphysical absolute, so that it is in the name of religious sentiment in its purity that such an object ought to be ruled out. There remains this hypothesis that, beyond the perspectives of knowledge, through which phenomenal reality is formulated in the indefinite of relation, there may be room for another form of existence in which the aspirations toward the absolute, perfection, justice and happiness, which are the characteristics of religious sensibility, would find their satisfaction. A philosophy of knowledge does not possess any datum authorizing it to deny this possibility.

132

Made to evolve in the world of relation it would, in such a matter, be as much in the wrong to deny as to affirm. Hence, in the absence of intellectual activity, desire, in the extreme form of faith, in which it transforms itself to the last degree of its intensity, is able to realize religious feeling in the belief in this other face of existence. The positive mind engendered by the philosophy of reason regards as one of its most precious intellectual conquests and as one of its clearest views the fact of having assigned a precise rank to a manifestation of human activity which, for all of being most often produced in mixed forms, none the less reveals so profound an aspiration that to ignore it or neglect it would proclaim the impotence of a philosophy. Then again one must not forget that the religious sentiment, which is here under consideration, is religious feeling in its purity and that any intellectual intervention tending to relate it to the phenomenal world, were it with a view to assigning a moral action to it, to attributing a meaning in terms of concepts, in images, in evocations borrowed from the phenomenal world, would indicate that it is a question of an imitation of religious sentiment, of a nature to arouse all suspicions, and not of religious feeling itself. If such a sentiment is felt without alteration by some isolated individuals belonging to the most diverse milieus in all religious confessions, or outside of any confession, it has never found collective expression except in the case of certain Buddhist monks. The latter made their entire religious symbol inhere in the mere accentuation of the syllable *om* devoid of any meaning, by which they affirmed nothing more than the rupture of any connection between the world conceived by their intelligence and the one which the fervor of their desire was realizing in an act of faith. But those monks belonged to the only philosophical race that ever was. The purity of their belief, situated in a region where no argument could contradict it, was based on that Brahminical metaphysics, compared with which our Judeo-

133

Hellenic Christian philosophies appear like tales for children and for the most simple-minded brains.

If the positive mind assigns to religious feeling in its purity a place, which cannot be disputed by any activity of the phenomenal order and which reconciles in sovereign fashion the play of this aspiration in its most radical form with the most diverse expressions of human life, it equally implies a very definite attitude with regard to the positive religions. Considering these religions as social facts, it is scarcely necessary to say that it need not give its attention to what the rationalistic philosophy would regard as their degree of truth. It can consider them only with respect to their social utility, that is to say their ability to create order in the human groups, which at one time or another adopted them. Already in the concluding chapter of my *De Kant à Nietzsche* I dealt with the rôle of religions in societies in the light of this positive point of view. In this brief exposition of a very general philosophy I can do no more than refer the reader interested in such viewpoints to those expositions. I shall only add here this final consideration: namely that, to the extent to which a religion formulates the rules of that general morality, which constitutes the condition of existence of a given social group, it must also be regarded as good in the measure in which it is believed to be true by the men of this group, its degree of social effectiveness proportioning itself to the degree of its influence.

This appraisement of the positive religions in terms of the degree of their efficacy and the valuation of this effectiveness in terms of the authority, of which they dispose over individuals can give some idea of the spirit, which inspired this criticism of official philosophy. The official

[1] *Métaphysiques et Morales au Point de Vue de la Connaissance.*

philosophy is a force. Represented by University philosophy, it is an organized force. Now it is contrary to the directions of the positive mind, as remote from revolutionary ideology as from conservative ideology, to ruin what in the human environment disposes of an efficient power of organization. It is, on the other hand, one of the aims of this study to contribute, in the domain of philosophical thought, to the advent of the positive spirit, whose substitution for the metaphysical mind would in itself attest that humanity is not at present in its period of regression, having on the wings of myth and fiction attained the limits of its possible greatness. Instead of ruining the credit of the official philosophy, it would be more advantageous to incline the power of expansion and the authority, of which it disposes, to play a rôle that could be considerable in the accomplishment of that metamorphosis, compared to which the most famous revolutions, the great historical convulsions and even the event of the last war would, in the history of the human species, be episodes of relatively minor importance. Now, if the University philosophy was not able to disengage itself from the influences of a past going back into scholasticism and into theology, it has still given evidence, in the course of these last thirty years, by the works of some of its representatives, of a fecundity and an originality of views, by which it has made an important contribution to the movement of ideas, of which philosophy ranges in a vast synthesis, exclusive of all compromise, the most diverse tendencies. It has done this in spite of the principles, which continue to guide it as a constituted corpus. By "philosophy" is meant this philosophy of knowledge and pure reason, which I have here opposed to the official rationalism. It is permissible to aver that, in the very ranks of the University, a certain number of minds are right now won over to this positive point of view, whose elaboration has for a hundred years formed the living part and the profound current of intellectual evolution and it

135

is perhaps not unreasonably venturous to think that a fairly slight shifting of the influences reigning in these milieus would be enough to determine the most felicitous metamorphoses. If such a hope is not marked with too much optimism, the official philosophy would then be confounded with philosophy. Receiving its clarity, it would communicate its force to it. The title of this study could change into this one, which I did not venture to give it: *The official philosophy. What it is, what it can be.*